Sacred G
The Mysteries of the Forest

Yvonne Aburrow

Sacred Grove
The Mysteries of the Forest

©1994 Yvonne Aburrow

ISBN 1 898307 12 1

First printed 1994
Reprinted June 1995
Reprinted Oct 1996

Cover design by Daryth Bastin
Cover Illustration by Simon Rouse

Published by:

Capall Bann Publishing
Ringway House
Kelvin Road
Newbury
Berks RG14 2DB

Tel/Fax 01635 46455

Contents

Hobby-horse

INTRODUCTION

"I was seeing in a sacred manner the shapes of all things in the spirit, and the shape of all things as they must live together, like one being. And I saw that the sacred hoop of my people was one of many hoops that made one circle, wide as daylight and as starlight, and in the centre grew one mighty flowering tree to shelter all the children of one mother and one father."

(Black Elk, of the Lakota)

The forest is the original home of humanity, and ultimately the source of all our dreams, myths, legends, and archetypes. When the first hunter-gatherers left the forest to become farmers, they took the earth mother and the vegetation god with them, adapted their legends to the cycle of the agricultural year, and prayed to them to make the crops grow. As technology grew more advanced and humans interacted with the environment in new ways, ancient deities took on new aspects.

As migrating peoples spread out east and west, they took their stories and their deities with them. As life became more complex, nomads became settled peoples, and invaders brought new gods and goddesses, the stories changed. However, the underlying archetypes which empowered the original myths are still recognisable in myths from widely divergent cultures: we are all part of "one circle, wide as daylight and as starlight".

The forest is the realm of the psyche and the feminine principle, a place of testing and initiation, of unknown perils and darkness. It is the underworld, the abode of the dead. In Norse mythology, one of the twelve dwellings of the gods was Ydalir, valley of yews, where Uller received the souls of the dead. Entering the Dark Forest or the Enchanted Forest is a threshold symbol. The soul enters the perils of the unknown, the realm of death, the secrets of nature or the spiritual world.

Retreat into the forest is a symbolic death before the rebirth of initiation. To the Hindus the forest dweller is one who has left the active world for a life of contemplation, who has 'died' to this world. This theme recurs in Norse sagas, medieval legends, and fairy tales; the hero retreats into the forest, where he undergoes a number of initiatory experiences, and re-emerges master of himself (or, in psychological terms, with his id, ego, and superego integrated). This is often represented as an exiled king, who regains his kingdom at the end of the story, or a young man, regarded as a simpleton, who undergoes many trials, wins the hand of the princess, and inherits the kingdom.

As might be expected, trees also play a significant part in ancient tales.

The tree represents the whole of manifestation, the synthesis of earth and water, and dynamic life. It is both imago mundi and axis mundi, joining the three worlds (heaven, earth, and underworld) and making communication between them possible. It gives access to the power of the sun; it is also an omphalos, a centre of dragon energy or cthonic power. It is the feminine principle, nourishing, sheltering, and protecting; trees are often depicted as female figures. As the world axis it is linked with the mountain and the pillar. The world tree is rooted in the depths of the earth at the centre of the world, and grows into the realm of Time, its branches representing differentiation on the plane of manifestation.

Enlightenment is achieved by identification with the World Tree, experiencing the absorption of mortal appearance in immortal being (Odin hanging on Yggdrasil, Christ on the Rood, Gautama Buddha sitting beneath the Bodhi Tree).

A tree with a serpent appears in many cultures. The tree is the cosmic axis; the serpent coiled round it is the cycles of manifestation. The same is true of the caduceus, Hermes' staff. Alternatively the serpent is the guardian of the tree, signifying the difficulty of getting wisdom, as in the case of the serpent Ladon which guarded the tree on which the Golden Apples of the Hesperides grew; or it may tempt the man or woman into eating the forbidden fruit, as in the Garden of Eden myth.

A tree with a stone and an altar is the moon tree. Often depicted with the moon, the tree symbolises the principle of change, the stone the principle of stasis. In ancient times, the body of a woman was the altar of the gods.

Climbing trees symbolises the ascent from one plane to another (e.g. achieving gnosis, ascending the Tree of Life in the Kabbalah).

Evergreen trees symbolise immortality and the undying spirit, and are often used in funerary and mourning rites to remind mourners of the resurrection or reincarnation to come (depending on your religious beliefs).

Deciduous trees represent renewal, regeneration, death and rebirth, resurrection, reproduction, and the life principle.

The journey of the inner self is intimately connected with tree imagery. Trees were once regarded as the ancestors of humanity, and it is the ancestral wisdom which guides the seeker after the Grail. The spirits of trees and other nature spirits can often be a source of help and inspiration in the quest. They are part of the sacred landscape which is the true Paradise. The ancients made themselves at home in new lands by mythologising the landscape; every tree, rock, hill, spring, pool, cavern, and river took on mythological associations.

> *"The manifestation of the sacred in a stone or a tree is neither less mysterious nor less noble than its manifestation as a 'god'. The process of sacralizing reality is the same; the forms taken by the process in man's religious consciousness differ."*
>
> *(Mircea Eliade, in "Shamanism: Archaic Techniques of Ecstasy", New York, 1948)*

It is this sacral quality of the landscape that modern humans urgently need to rediscover. As the sacred places of Britain are despoiled by materialist barbarians, more and more people are becoming aware of the need to defend them. The Dongas defended Twyford Down from the onslaught of the Department of Transport; Oxleas Wood has been saved; now there is a protest on Solsbury Hill, near Bath, against a road being built there. Trees and hills and standing stones are sacred, and the island of Britain would be immeasurably poorer in spirit without them. They are the foci of earth energies, the sources of mythical renewal.

This book is dedicated to all those who hold the land sacred, and all those who are defending the Earth from those who would despoil her.

The Initiation in the Forest

Initiates have always sought enlightenment in the forest; many tales tell of the questing hero in the forest. There are few tales of the questing heroine, but such tales do exist.

We originated in the forest, and must return there to find the lost half of our consciousness. The quest is different for the man and the woman, however. It is probable that woman invented agriculture, and hence settlement and civilisation; whilst the men were out hunting, the women experimented with growing crops. So the man must come from the forest and enter the citadel of the soul to awaken the sleeping princess, his anima. The woman must leave the citadel and enter the forest to find the wild man of the woods, her animus. They then find the complementary other half which will enable them to function fully as human beings.

Fairy stories are a rich source of archetypal imagery. The heroes and heroines of fairy tales are never fully rounded characters; they are archetypes. Fairy tales awaken the child within all of us; for children instinctively understand the psychological truth of fairy tales. They are still capable of 'the willing suspension of disbelief' which is necessary to the understanding of any drama.

The Greeks used masks to emphasise the mythical nature of their dramas; in fairy tales the device used is that the characters do not have names like ordinary mortals, but are described by their distinguishing characteristic, e.g. Snow White, Sleeping Beauty, etc. The only apparent exception to this is Jack (best known from the story of Jack and the Beanstalk), but in every story in which he appears, he is the simpleton who triumphs over his adversary where cleverer men have failed, because he lives the life of instinct. (The importance of the life of instinct is pointed out in Benjamin Hoff's excellent book, "The Tao of Pooh".)

According to Bruno Bettelheim in "The Uses of Enchantment", children relate to fairy stories by identifying with the hero or heroine. However, for adults, who have lost much of the imagination of the child, a more direct method is needed. A very effective method is the use of visualisation. I have written two visual journeys, one for men and one for women. The women's visualisation is loosely based on a story I vaguely remember reading as a child - I think it was called "The Golden Ball". The men's visualisation is based on the story of "The Sleeping Beauty", seen from the point of view of the prince who comes to awaken the sleeping princess.

Visualisations can be done in groups or alone. If you are doing it alone, the best way is to memorise the gist of the visualisation beforehand, and to embark upon your journey in a quiet room. If you are working in a group, one person should read the visualisation out to the others (preferably having done it themselves alone earlier, and read the script through a few times to get the emphasis right) slowly, rhythmically, and meaningfully. The use of tape recorders is not recommended, as the tinny effect of a recorded voice, the hissing of the tape, and the turning of the spools, are all irritating distractions. What is needed is someone with an almost hypnotic voice, who can modulate their tone appropriately for the sense of a passage - and a tape detracts from the effect of even the best reader. Incidentally, if you are doing the Sleeping Beauty visualisation with a group, don't tell them that it is the story of Sleeping Beauty - that way you get an element of surprise, which should always be incorporated into an initiatory experience.

The Golden Ball (visualisation for women)

Standing in the temple of the mind, you see a small golden pentagram hanging in the darkness. As you look at it, it grows larger, until it becomes the size of a door. It is filled with a golden mist. You reach out to touch the frame, and as you do so the mist clears, and you can step through into a sunlit garden, filled with the scent of oranges. The bright fruit hang like small suns amongst the dark green leaves of the trees, forming a contrast with the ochre stonework of the wall, encrusted with lichen and warmed by the sun. You are walking towards a patio, feeling rather uncomfortable in a stiff brocade dress.

On the patio are several other women, some embroidering, some spinning. You take your place amongst the women, embroidering on a tapestry stretched on a frame. Your brothers are practising for the forthcoming tournament in the courtyard, and their shouts echo from the castle walls. Feeling somewhat bored, you stand up and go out onto the lawn amongst the trees. Taking a golden ball from your pocket, you begin to bounce it against the wall, catching it as it rebounds. But one throw is too high, and the golden ball sails over the wall. "Damn," you exclaim, and proceed to remove the stiff dress so that you are dressed only in a linen shift. Then you climb the nearest orange tree, hitching the shift up around your knees, and scramble onto the top of the wall. It is a dizzying jump down to the ground on the other side, but the ground rises away from the wall, so you close your eyes and make a flying leap, landing in a heap in the grass on the other side. Unhurt, you stand up, and head into the forest, which begins only a few yards from the castle wall.

Once inside the forest, it is cool, and silent but for the whispering of the trees. Animals rustle in the undergrowth, and once a startled pheasant whirrs up from the path in front of you. The crashing of a wild boar can be heard in a distant thicket. Your search for the golden ball continues, however, for you are undaunted by these things, being a real woman. You walk on through the forest, searching for a glint of gold in the undergrowth, but there is no sign of the ball. Eventually you decide to give up the search and go home, so you turn round and head for the castle. But now it seems that the forest is playing tricks on you - surely you passed that tree a minute ago? You find yourself going round in circles, trying to find your way back. And now dusk is falling, and the undergrowth seems more menacing, forming the shapes and contours of demons.

You are just about to prepare to bivouac for the night when you see a glimmer of light through the trees. Heading towards it, you find your way impeded by brambles tearing at your clothes, but you press on, and eventually emerge into a glade. There is a small fire pointing its beacon of light at the stars, and seated at the fire is the wildest-looking man you have ever seen. He is naked but for a golden torc about his neck and a cloak made of pelts around his shoulders. His hair is entwined with leaves - holly, ivy, oak, ash, and thorn. His eyes sparkle in the firelight - or is it the freedom of the woods which gives them their radiance? He is wild and menacing in aspect, but has an air of mischief about him. He looks at you as you enter the glade, and you see that he is tossing your golden ball from one hand to the other, apparently fascinated by the gleaming sphere. "Ah, Princess," he greets you. "Have you lost something?"

"I had lost that golden ball which you have in your hands," you reply.

"What will you do to have this golden ball again?" he asks, musingly.

"I will kill you if you do not give it to me," you reply.

He laughs. You feel a bit sheepish.

"I will give you a kiss if you will give me the ball," you try again.

He laughs at you again. "I have a better plaything for you, Princess," he says, and stands up.

"Come with me," he says. You follow, somewhat reluctantly, out of the clearing and along a path, until you come to a rocky outcrop, whose folds hide the entrance to a cave. The entrance is overhung with creepers, and the cave is very dark. As your eyes become accustomed to the dark, you see that the man is an alchemist. Various alembics stand on shelves and in niches, and herbs hang from the ceiling. Books and papers are spread over a large table, along with various instruments for charting the movements of the stars: an astrolabe, an orrery, and other esoterica.

The man goes to a chest at the back of the cave, and takes out a knife with a black handle. He gives it to you, hilt first. The handle is carved with signs, and the steel blade glitters in the darkness. It is a knife of great power. Thanking him, you draw a pentagram in the still night air, which grows larger and larger, until you can step through it, back into the temple of your mind.

Gradually the room forms around you again, but you know that you can return again whenever you wish to visit your wild man of the woods.

The Sleeping Beauty (visualisation for men)

Standing in the temple of the mind, you can see a small silver pentagram hanging in the darkness. As you look at it, it starts to grow larger, and as it grows, it fills with mist. Soon it is the size of a door, and you reach out to touch the silver frame. As you do so, the mists clear, and you are able to step through into a beautiful spring evening. The birds are singing all about you, and the grass is covered with dew. But the place has an unkempt look, and there are brambles trailing everywhere. The air is full of the scent of roses, but there is a disturbing undertone to the scent which you cannot identify - until you see a skull lying in the grass, a rose-tendril snaking through one empty eye socket. Here and there amongst the undergrowth, there lies a rusty sword or a piece of armour.

You walk forward, unscathed by the brambles, for you are clad in light silver armour, with a surtout emblazoned with the Moon and the sign of Venus. As you push through the brambles, you find that they part for you as if by magic, though a few of the long cruel thorns pierce your mail-gloved hand and draw blood. Here and there a rosebud adorns the brambles, its curvaceous shape and slightly parted lips allowing a glimpse of the beauty within. the great trees of the ancient forest brood silently above you, their huge trunks grey-green in the mysterious evening light. The massive banks of brambles threaten to engulf you, as their trailing thorny branches arch overhead.

But at last you emerge from the brambles, and a breathtaking sight awaits you. A huge Gothic castle rises up out of the mists. Slender turrets crowned with pointed roofs jostle with crumbling stonework, overgrown with moss and ivy. They give the splendid castle an ancient air, as if nothing had stirred there for a hundred years. The walls are surmounted with great gargoyles, grimacing horribly, and they frighten you with their empty staring eyes. But you put aside your fear, for you have penetrated the thickets of thorns, though they drew blood from you. So you walk resolutely towards the portcullis of the mysterious castle. It is strange and eerie, though, no guards patrol the walls, and no-one is at the gate. But as you approach, an old woman emerges from the shadows of the dark portal. She is dressed in black robes, and leans upon a knotted stick. She is hooded, but under the hood is a face both ancient and yet eternally young. It is a wise face, with lines set in it by both tears and laughter. She smiles at you. You may be surprised at her benevolence, for she is an object of fear and scorn because she is a woman of power, and many lies have been told about her.

When she speaks, her voice is a whisper like leaves borne on the wind, but it is awesome and powerful. "Welcome, Prince," she says. "What do you seek in the castle of the Briar Rose?"

"I seek enlightenment and healing, ancient one," you reply.

"Then you are welcome to the citadel of the soul," she answers, and stands aside so that you may pass through the dread portal. As you walk through, you bow to her, and she gives you a candle in a silver sconce. You thank her, and stand for a moment awed by the vastness of the place. It takes a while for your eyes to become accustomed to the darkness, but when they do, you can see a wide staircase ahead. You walk slowly across the cold flagstones of the hall, stepping carefully to avoid treading on the sleeping guards and servants.

Cobweb-bedecked suits of armour maintain a ghostly vigil on the stairs. You walk up the stairs, feeling the smooth stonework of the balustrade. At the top of the stairs you find a wooden door standing ajar, and with beating heart you open it wide to find a winding spiral staircase. Your candle flickers in the draught as you walk up it. At the top there is another wooden door, which opens on a small room with a huge four-poster bed hung with red velvet curtains. Stretched out on the bed, abandoned to sleep, is the most beautiful woman you have ever seen. Illuminated by the friendly moonlight, her face has the pearly insubstantial beauty of the soul; yet it is also the tangible beauty of the earth in winter, the rosebud of infinite tenderness, terrible and beautiful. She wears a flowing white gown embroidered with pearls, and the bed is strewn with rosepetals. Their scent fills the room. There is a look of sadness in her face, as if she had known great sorrow and suffering. This enhances her beauty, and tugs at your heartstrings, so that you rush forward to kiss her, for she is the very image of the Goddess. As you kiss her silent face, the room swirls and melts away. The castle vanishes, and you find yourself standing in a beautiful garden, full of the scents of summer.

The awakened Beauty stands before you, her eyes dancing with merriment. She is clad in the green gown of Venus, and a star-like gem is bound upon her brow with a silver fillet. Flowers spring up under her feet as she walks, and you follow her to a glade where nymphs and satyrs are dancing. There, two thrones stand empty, and the Beauty leads you by the hand to sit with her. Joining hands, you sit on the throne. The nymphs and satyrs come to crown you with garlands of roses, and dance joyously and madly about the glade. Amongst them you recognise the faces of the servants you saw sleeping in the hall.

The old woman in black appears on the margin of the forest, watching the festivities and smiling. With her staff, she draws the pentagram on the edge of the forest. Once more, it grows to the size of a door, and you and the beauty step through it, returning to the here and now. The room where you are sitting forms again around you, and the glade fades from view, becoming at last a tiny miniature within the pentagram.

The Fire in the Glade: The Art of Story-telling

Hear, my beloved, an old Milesian story! -
High, and embosom'd in congregated laurels,
Glimmer'd a temple upon a breezy headland;
In the dim distance amid the skiey billows
Rose a fair island; the god of flocks had blest it.
From the far shores of the bleat-resounding island
Oft by the moonlight a little boat came floating,
Came to the sea-cave beneath the breezy headland,
Where amid myrtles a pathway stole in mazes
Up to the grove of the high embosom'd temple.
There in a thicket of dedicated roses,
Oft did a priestess, as lovely as a vision,
Pouring her soul to the son of Cytherea,
Pray him to hover around the slight canoe-boat,
And with invisible pilotage to guide it
Over the dusk wave, until the nightly sailor
Shivering with ecstasy sank upon her bosom.

(S. T. Coleridge)

There is an art to story-telling, but it is something of which everyone is capable under the right conditions. Many people are embarrassed if they are asked to perform in public, so the circumstances must be made as intimate as possible. If telling stories out of doors, find a glade or sheltered spot where you will not be disturbed. If possible, go there at night and light a fire; there is something particularly archaic and inspiring about firelight. If you are telling stories indoors, turn out any electric lights and fill the room with candles. Again, it provides an inspiring atmosphere. It is best to start with some sort of working to build up energy. This can be a simple meditation on the four elements, or drumming and dancing to transform consciousness. The energy raised could be focussed onto a group totem, from which all present can draw inspiration.

When beginning story-telling sessions, it is best for everyone to prepare a story for performance beforehand. Learning a story verbatim, however, will not allow creativity to flow; the gist of it can be learnt, and the details will emerge in the telling. This is very difficult to begin with, but the response of your audience will make it easier as time goes on. Incidentally, it is better if any audience participation is constructive - awkward questions tend to break the spell.

When you have reached the stage where everyone is comfortable with performing stories, you can begin to devise new plots and characters, or tell old stories from a different viewpoint. You could also accompany the tale with music (a sistrum, a bow harp, or a tabor), perhaps even with mime. You might even manage to start forming your tale into rhyming couplets, as you access the rhythmic elements of right-brain functioning. The feeling of being taken over by a story which demands to be told is incredible - it is accessing a different level of consciousness, where the archetypes roam in the twilit caverns of the collective unconscious.

I have given some examples of tales which relate to the mysteries of the forest. Poetry is also meant to be performed, and is a sacred art in its own right. Poets and story-tellers were respected for their shamanic abilities, as transformers of consciousness.

A successful story has more than one level of meaning; it can be taken literally and symbolically. This is why fairy tales are so successful, because they address real life issues in terms of our symbolic relation to them, and their heroes and heroines are archetypal, so clearly stand for aspects of the psyche. Myths, on the other hand, are played out with a tragic inevitability in which humans are powerless to intervene. They serve a different purpose; they are cathartic, that is, inspiring pity and terror so profound that the psyche is released to spiritual rapture.

Some tales from the forest

The Devil's Instrument

There was once a family of Romani, who dwelt in the forests of the Balkans. A deep melancholy shrouded the forest, and all was silent and still. Occasionally the silence was broken by the wail of a child or the cry of a rejected lover. For one of the daughters of the tribe was a chohawni, a witch, and she was very beautiful. Her name was Mara. But her eyes were cruel, and her demeanour was haughty. Many of the young men of the tribe had declared their love for her, but she had rejected them all, and slept alone in her tent.

One day, as she walked through the winter-shrouded forest, she saw a weasel crossing her path, and knew that some ill-luck was about to befall her. She forgot all about it the very next instant, though, when she saw the most handsome young man she had ever set eyes on walking through the forest. He was a gadjo hunter, one of the young men from the plains. His moustache curled over his lip, and his eyes seemed to pierce her to her soul. She longed for him to take her in his arms, and yet could not believe that this handsome young man would take any notice of her. She managed to compose herself sufficiently to emerge from the trees and walk towards him, but he affected not to notice her; all he saw was a wild gipsy girl, and he did not notice her beauty.

Over the next few weeks, however, the gadjo hunter continued to seek for game in the forest, and Mara followed him, watching his every movement with the hunger of unrequited love. But he spurned her affections, and she despaired of ever winning his love.

Eventually her yearning became so intense that she summoned up the Devil, and begged him to help her win the heart of the hunter. He agreed, but demanded that she give him her mother, father, and four brothers as payment. She agreed, and the Devil fashioned the father into a sound-box, the four brothers into strings, and the mother into a bow. The melancholy sound produced by this instrument was the lamentations of the family. Mara took it, and with the help of its wild music, seduced the gadjo hunter. But they had only one night of passion before the Devil reappeared and carried them off to Hell. The violin that he had made was left lying on the ground in the forest. Eventually a poor Gipsy picked it up and spent the winter learning to play it. Then he went from village to village, playing haunting melodies and wild dance music, sometimes singing of his life.

Na janav ko dad m'ro has,	I have never known my father,
niko mallen mange has;	and I lack friends;
Miro gule dai merdyas,	My mother is long dead
Pirani man pregelyas;	And my loved one departed angry;
Uva tu, oh hegedive,	You only, oh violin,
Tut sal minding pash mange...	Accompany me in the world...
The m're vodyi man dukhal,	Let my heart break with grief,
Posici cuces tu sal,	I hear no money in my pocket,
Papel ma bashavav,	I play a tune on my violin,
Paletunes pashlovyav...	And silence hunger and grief...
Uva tu, oh hegedive,	You only, oh violin,
Tut sal minding pash mange...	Accompany me in the world...

M'ra shatrako hin duy malla	My violin has two friends
Mange, pera, vodyi cavlya:	Who eat my very marrow:
Kamaviben te piben	Love and Hunger,
Taysa hin pash bash	They accompany me, a musician...
bashapen...	

Rotkäppchen

As a child, I was always regarded as fey. My mother was a
devout Christian, and attended Mass regularly. But the priest
and the people always looked askance at me, saying that I
spent too much time with my grandmother, and often seemed
to be seeing things that were not there. My mother was
ashamed of my grandmother, and told me never to stray from
the true path of Christianity. She said the Old Religion was
the worship of idols and devils. I knew that she had
abandoned it at an early age, I and would often ask my
grandmother to teach me her lore. She would always tell me
to wait until I was older, but she gave me a little red cap in
token that I belonged to the Old Religion. I wore it always, so
that it earned me the nickname of Little Red Riding Hood.

One day, when my mother had gone to church, I slipped out of
the house with a basket of food for my grandmother, and set
off for her cottage, which was deep in the heart of the forest.
On the way I gathered herbs of medicinal virtue, and whistled
snatches of old songs. The fly agaric mushrooms with their red
caps seemed to glow faintly under the birch trees, and the
birds sang of the coming winter.

As I came to the wildwood, there was a clap of thunder. I
heard a hue and cry, and saw a troop of hunters in full pursuit
of a wolf. The hounds were of many different shapes and sizes,
and some of the hunters seemed to be wounded. Following the
mounted troop was a creaking cart, driven by a youth of

startling ferocity. I hurried to my grandmother's cottage, not knowing the meaning of this strange apparition. The door was open, and I went in.

My grandmother was sitting by the fire, tending a pot of herbs on the hearth. The wolf was stretched out on the kitchen floor, panting heavily. I backed away, but my grandmother reassured me that the wolf was harmless. I told her what I had seen, and she smiled. She told me that I was ready to begin my apprenticeship in the Craft of the Wise. Then there was a tap at the window. It was the youth who had been driving the cart. He was clad in wolfskin, and had antlers growing from his forehead. To my surprise, the wolf got up and went out to him, and my grandmother motioned to me to do likewise.

We found the wild cavalcade waiting for us, and climbed up onto the cart. As the procession began again, accompanied by the wild music of drums and pipes, the earth beneath us fell away and we were travelling on the paths of the winds. Streamers of cloud wrapped themselves around us like wraiths, and the cold night air turned our faces blue. At last we came to a great black mountain at the end of the world, where there were many witches dancing naked. Some of them were in the form of magpies, some were hares, and some were geese. Stags, wolves, bears, and cats ran amongst the throng, and I seemed to recognise people I had thought long dead. We danced under the full Moon until at last I dropped, exhausted, to the ground.

When I reawakened, I was in bed in my grandmother's house, and she was snoring peacefully in the next room. Later that night I discovered with my fingers another little red cap, which has ever since transported me to the realms of the unseen.

King Herla

Herla was king over the Ancient Britons. One day he was challenged by another king, who was a pigmy no bigger than an ape. This king rode on a large goat, and wore a spotted fawn skin. He had a large head, glowing face, and a long red beard. He was rough and hairy, with the hooves of a goat. He told Herla that he was king over a vast and innumerable people. Then he praised Herla's renown, and said that they were related by both blood and position. He then told him that the King of France was sending Herla an envoy offering his daughter in marriage, and proposed an everlasting treaty, because he was at Herla's marriage, and Herla would attend his marriage on the same day a year from hence.

The embassy from France arrived just as predicted, and Herla assented to their proposals. When the marriage was celebrated, the pigmies arrived, bringing jewelled cups and wonderful food. A year later, Herla went to the marriage of the dwarf king. They entered a cave in a high cliff, and after journeying through the earth, they came to the dwarf's palace. There the marriage was celebrated, and Herla was loaded with gifts, horses, dogs, hawks, and everything necessary for hunting and falconry. Then the pigmy guided them back down the dark tunnel, and gave them a bloodhound small enough to be carried. He strictly forbade any of Herla's retinue to dismount until the dog leapt down from the man carrying him, then said goodbye and returned home.

When they came out into daylight, they returned to Herla's kingdom, and found an old shepherd. Herla asked for news of his queen, but the shepherd looked at him in astonishment. He said that he could scarcely understand his speech, for Herla was a Briton and he was a Saxon, and that he had had heard of that lady as the wife of an ancient king called Herla, who was believed to have disappeared into that cliff, never to be seen again. The Saxons had ruled over that country for two hundred years, having driven out the Britons. Herla was astounded, for he thought he had only been away for three days. Then some of his companions, forgetting the dwarf's instructions, dismounted, and instantly crumbled to dust. Herla then told the rest of his companions not to dismount until the dog had leapt down. The dog has not leapt down yet. King Herla is said to wander with his company on mad journeys without end or rest. In the first year of the reign of Henry II, however, the Welsh reported that they had seen Herla and his company washed away in the River Wye, and their strange wanderings finally ceased.

The Wonderful Wood

There was once a cruel king who liked to hunt young maidens, and after he had caught them and had his wicked way with them, he would kill them with his sword. All the mothers and fathers in the kingdom sent their daughters away if they could, to escape this cruel fate, but there was one little girl who could not go. Her granny was too poor to send her, so she kept her hidden in their lonely cottage, and earned enough to feed them both with her spinning.

Near the cottage was a wonderful wood with a great oak tree in it. Everyone, including the cruel king, was afraid to go there. One day the granny was ill, so the little girl had to take the wool to market, or they would starve. They both cried and kissed each other, and the granny told her to go on tiptoes all the way, but not to go through the wonderful wood, although it was the quickest way. So the little girl went off with the bundle of wool, but she had not got very far before she saw the cruel king riding on horseback in the distance.

She went into the wonderful wood and curtsied to the oak tree, and the oak tree let her pass safely through the wood to the town. But the cruel king had seen her go, and he spurred on his horse and rode after her into the wood. When he came to the oak tree, he cursed at it, and drew his sword to kill the little girl, but a bough fell from the tree and broke his neck. Then the king's men came looking for him, and seeing him lying dead on the ground, rode into the forest to cut down the tree.

> "O they rode in the wood where the oaken tree stood,
> To cut down the tree, the oaken tree,
> Then the tree gave a groan and summoned his own,
> For the trees closed about and they never got out
>   Of the wood, the wonderful wood."

(The stories given above are my own retellings of traditional stories. More folk tales can be found in the many published collections of folk tales. Particularly recommended are: "A Dictionary of British Folk-Tales", Vols. 1 & 2, by Katharine M. Briggs, Routledge and Kegan Paul, 1970; and "British Folk Tales: new versions", by Kevin Crossley-Holland, Orchard Books, 1987.)

The Oak King and The Holly King

Chapter 1

THE HISTORY OF TREES IN THE BRITISH ISLES

After the retreat of the last Ice Age (8300 - 8200 BCE), trees began to colonise Britain. At that time Britain was still connected to mainland Europe. Gradually the trees spread over the land, advancing over the areas left by the retreating ice, creating the wildwood which for a long time covered the whole of Britain. The first trees to colonise Britain were juniper and birch, followed by pine (7500 BCE), which pushed birch into highland areas. The progress of various species can be determined by dating pollen deposits in the soil. Juniper, birch, and pine, were followed by hazel, elm, oak, alder, and, some time later, small-leaved lime.

For the next two thousand years these trees established themselves in Britain, and are now known as our indigenous species. Around fifty to seventy other species also arrived during this period. Mesolithic hunters interfered little with this process. However, they did use fire to burn forests, though they were hunter-gatherer peoples with no agriculture. They also domesticated the dog.

Around 5500 BCE, Britain became separated from mainland Europe by the English Channel, so no more trees could colonise the land.

The commonest trees in the wildwood varied from one region to another. Birch and pine were commonest in the Scottish Highlands; oak and hazel in the Scottish Lowlands, the North of England, and North and Mid Wales; hazel and elm in South-West Wales and Cornwall; and small-leaved lime in the Midlands and Home Counties. Beech had reached southern England by 3000 BCE. The wildwood was not necessarily dense and impenetrable. Grass and hazel pollen have been found; neither of these plants will flower properly in shade. Hornbeam is indigenous only to parts of southern England and Wales.

Around 3100 - 2900 BCE, there was a marked decline in numbers of elms, probably due to the arrival of Neolithic humans, who farmed herd animals, which may have browsed young elm shoots, or the people may have gathered the shoots for fodder. Alternatively elms may have been attacked by disease. The knowledge of sowing and reaping crops spread to the Neolithic people of Britain from the Near East. They began to build tombs and stone circles, and developed flint mining at sites like Grimes Graves in Norfolk.

As the Neolithic era (5000 - 2000 BCE) merged into the Bronze Age (1700 - 500 BCE), large areas of land were converted to fields for crops or for grazing. Pines entirely disappeared from England and Wales at this point (they burn easily, and do not coppice or sucker - that is, sprout from stumps or grow again from roots). It is possible that Neolithic people knew how to coppice (cut trees back to the stump to make them grow clumps of straight poles). "Corduroy roads" (pole tracks across bogs) were pre- Roman; the earliest has been dated at 3174 BCE. It is probable that the knowledge of smelting bronze (an alloy of copper and tin) was brought to Britain by the Beaker People, who arrived around 2200 BCE.

Around 400 BCE, the Celts arrived in Britain with iron ploughs, which could manage the heavy clay soil of valleys, hitherto left wooded. They also needed wood to smelt iron, and had discovered enamelling.

When the Romans came on the scene, they cleared a lot of woodland to produce grain during their occupation. The first Roman expedition to Britain was around 100 BCE. The Romans invaded Britain in 43 BCE; their occupation lasted until around 400 CE. They built roads, towns, villas, and forts. They were mostly Pagan until around 250 CE. Many of the Celtic aristocracy became Romanised, and adopted Christianity when the Romans did. In Wales and the Scottish borders, a lot of trees were cleared for military purposes. The Romans also introduced industry, smelting and forging iron in the Sussex Weald and the Forest of Dean; smelting lead in Derbyshire. Their cities and settlements needed wood as fuel for heating and cooking and their country villas needed it to heat their baths and hypocausts. An analysis of Roman charcoal suggests that coppiced woodland provided a regular supply of fuel. When the Romans departed, the trees returned to some areas, but they were often cleared again by the Saxons.

Whereas the Romans had used a lot of stone, the Saxons built with timber. Therefore they needed large trees for frames and beams, as well as smaller trees for posts, studs, and panels of wattle infilling. They continued to coppice woodland for small timber.

The first recorded use of the perambulation was in Saxon times. The perambulation was written in a charter which defined the extent of a piece of land by describing a walk around its boundaries.

The introduction of a more feudal way of life by the Normans necessitated a survey of their new kingdom. The Domesday Book was completed in 1086 CE, and provides a useful picture of the land at that time. The woods of some counties were described by area, others by dimensions, and others only by their worth when rented out for pannage (to fatten pigs), or by the number of pigs which could be grazed there, so it is difficult to calculate how much woodland there was. The Forest of Dean was left blank, so it was probably still mostly wildwood. William the Conqueror laid claim to large tracts of forest as royal hunting preserves (the Saxon Kings had had hunting rights beyond the royal demesne, but they were not exclusive). Forest law was established in these areas, ensuring the protection of game and trees from all but the King, who had sole hunting, felling, and mineral rights. However, he could and did lease them to others. Denizens of the forest could only fell wood for their personal use, and were not allowed to assart the land (convert it to agricultural use). Forest law was first defined by a statute of 1184 known as the Assize of Woodstock.

Ecological historians generally express doubt that there is any wildwood left in Britain; that is, trees actually surviving from a time when virgin forest covered Britain. What were probably the last of these in England were destroyed when 71 giant oaks from the Forest of Dean were sold by Henry III to the Dominican friary at Gloucester between 1241 and 1265 CE. If, however, wildwood is defined as an area of ground continuously covered by trees since the last Ice Age, it seems surprising that there are no such areas. There was a tradition that Wistman's Wood on Dartmoor was prehistoric, but this has now been proved false. The situation was certainly different in Scotland, where there was plenty of stone to build with and peat for fuel. The Scottish wildwood remained undisturbed till around 1600 CE. As late as 1830, some large decayed trees were found in Glenmore in Inverness-shire, which may have been part of an undisturbed piece of woodland.

An excellent fictional account of the magical properties of the wildwood can be found in Robert Holdstock's novel "Mythago Wood", and the sequel, "Lavondyss". The novel recounts the experiences of a man whose father discovers that the tract of wildwood near his home harbours 'mythagos' (myth images) which are archetypal figures produced by the interaction of the collective unconscious of the inhabitants of Britain, and the consciousness of the trees and the land. The wood itself functions as a kind of vortex of power, and the further into the wood one goes, the more powerful the mythagos.

In medieval times, woodland was recognised to be a valuable resource. The highest value was placed on fully-coppiced woods, but it was generally the practice to intersperse coppice stools with standards (fully mature trees) to be used for timber-framed houses and other large structures. Most of these were oaks, which were usually cut at around seventy years of age.

Wood from coppices was used for charcoal to smelt and forge iron, for sticks, wattle, hurdles, domestic fuel, etc. It is possible to coppice ash, lime, oak, hazel, maple, and wych elm. Coppice shoots will grow up to 11 feet high in the first year, and may be harvested at intervals of between four and sixty years. Some ancient coppice stools are up to 15 feet wide. They spread as they get older because new shoots grow in a ring round the outside of previous growth. One ash stool in East Anglia is reckoned to be over a thousand years old. Elm and aspen do not coppice when felled, but they do sucker (grow again from the roots), producing clones, which may be harvested at intervals of between four and sixty years. Pollarding trees (cutting them with an axe at a height of between 6 and 15 feet) was rarer, because it entailed more effort. In East Anglia, willows are often pollarded.

The rights of various people to use woodland were carefully defined, and rents were paid for these rights, which had legal names: pannage (feeding pigs); herbage (feeding other animals); firebote (collecting firewood); haybote (collecting wood for hedging); and housebote (collecting wood for house repairs).

The decline of woodland has often been blamed on iron smelting, but it is unlikely to be the culprit, as smelting and forging relied on wood as a renewable resource from coppiced and pollarded trees, to make charcoal. In any case, the iron industry went into decline in the seventeenth century, due to competition from Sweden, which had developed better techniques; and in the eighteenth century, charcoal smelting became obsolete when Abraham Darby invented coke smelting.

The major cause of the decline of woodland was agriculture. Animals grazed in the woods, eating young shoots and thereby preventing new trees from growing. When enclosures were widely enforced, this marginal land was the obvious choice, and it was often converted to pasture or arable land by felling trees. However, industry took its toll on trees. Between 1550 and 1700, the glass industry used a lot of wood. In the early nineteenth century, the tanning industry used a lot of oak bark. Until the eighteenth century when brick became more common, the main house-building material was timber. Ship-building also used a lot of timber, but it probably had less impact than the tanning industry. Standard trees would have been needed for ships and houses, but some of the other industries only required coppiced trees, which were renewable.

The decline in woodland began to be recognised in the late fifteenth and early sixteenth centuries. In 1482, a statute was passed allowing owners of woods to fence them for seven years after they had been coppiced, to allow new shoots time to grow. In 1543, a statute of Henry VIII ordered that all woods must be enclosed for four years after coppicing, and at least 12 standard trees left standing in every acre. Tree planting for timber began in England in the late sixteenth century (earlier in Scotland), and continued in the eighteenth and nineteenth centuries. Planting increased dramatically after 1919, when the Forestry Commission was established. According to Lloyd

George, Britain nearly lost the First World War for lack of timber, not lack of food as is generally supposed.

Forest animals

The prehistoric forests of Britain harboured bears and lions; they were probably extinct by the time of the Norman Conquest.

The king's game (protected species) were the 'beasts of the forest': fallow deer (imported by the Normans), and red deer, roe deer, and wild boar. The meat of all four species was called venison.

Other animals (wolves, badgers, foxes, martens, wild cats, otters, hares, rabbits, and squirrels) were also hunted, but were not protected by law. Outside the royal forests anyone could hunt them, except in areas where free-warren (the right to hunt them) had been exclusively granted to an individual or an institution.

Wolves were common until the thirteenth century, and probably died out in the reign of Henry VII. What was probably the last wolf in the British Isles was killed in Scotland in 1743.

Further reading: Alan Fairhurst and Eric Soothill, "Trees of the Countryside", Blandford 1989 and Thomas Hinde, "Forests of Britain" Gollancz, 1985.

The Green Man

Chapter 2

THE INNER REALM OF PRYDAIN:
Folklore, Legend, Customs, Folk Heroes, and Folk Song

Folklore relating to trees touched on all aspects of country life. Cattle, horses, sheep, dairies, orchards, and the home all had various protective woods, and other woods which must not come into contact with them.

Blossom

If flowers and fruit appear together on the apple tree, it is said to be a portent of a death in the family. It is unlucky to bring unseasonal blossom into the house. Lilac bushes were said to go into mourning and not to flower if one of their number was felled.

It was unlucky to bring various tree blossom indoors: blackthorn, apple, plum, pear, hawthorn, and elder were all unlucky. It was permissible, however, to bring hawthorn blossom into the house on May Day. In Suffolk, the first servant to bring a spray of creamy hawthorn blossom into the house was given a dish of cream for breakfast. This custom died out after the calendar reform of 1752, as hawthorn was then rarely in bloom on May 1st.

It was unlucky to bring broom (the plant) into the house in May, especially if it was in flower:

"Bring broom into the house in May,
It will sure sweep one of the family away." (1868)

The House

Elder trees were grown by the house door to ward off harmful magic. Black Fenland adders were often found curled round the roots of elder trees, enhancing their reputation as a magical tree. In Somerset a wreath of flowers was hung on the nearest ash tree to the farm to ward off snakebite for a year. (Snakes are said to be frightened of ash trees, so making an offering to the tree would procure its protection. On May Eve it was customary to put birch and rowan branches over the house doors "to keep witches away", as witches were especially powerful on May Eve.)

Rowan trees were also planted at cottage doors for protection, and rowan twigs were built into church walls for protection. Rowan twigs are tied in an equal-armed cross with red thread (the twigs must be removed from the tree without the use of a knife). The Scottish Highlanders sewed these into the lining of their clothes, and Cornish people carried them in their pockets to protect them from sorcery. In Lincolnshire the rowan is used to deflect the spells of malevolent male sorcerers. Rowan wands are placed over the door on quarter days to ensure good fortune; at Beltane they are combined with birch twigs to bring good fortune and fertility for the whole year, and placed over door lintels. Rowan wood was carried on ships to prevent storms and kept in the house to guard against lightning strikes; it is placed on graves to ensure that the spirit of the deceased will have rest. Rowan trees growing near stone circles are reputed to be the most magically potent. Speer-posts, magically protective house-timbers inscribed with runes and magical patterns, were made of rowan-wood.

Holly trees were planted outside the house to ward off lightning, harmful magic, evil spirits, and poison. Larch was used as a charm against fire. An equal-armed cross of oak twigs bound with red thread was hung in the house to ward off evil. Oak timber was included in buildings to ward off lightning, particularly wood from a tree which had already been struck by lightning, as it was believed that lightning never struck the same tree twice. The festive Yuletide holly and ivy could not be brought into the house until Christmas Eve, otherwise it was unlucky; similarly mistletoe could not be brought into the house until New Year's Day. Afterwards, the holly must be burned; it would be disrespectful to throw it away. In the North of England, however, it was thought extremely unlucky to burn it! In Wales, the Isle of Man, and Peel, the holly and ivy were kept hanging on the walls until Candlemas, and burnt in the fire on which the pancakes were made on Shrove Tuesday. It was also regarded as very unlucky to cut down a holly tree.

To ward off the Wild Hunt, a pair of antlers was fixed to the outside of the house.

The bay tree was regarded as a lucky tree; an elderly Buckinghamshire lady moving house in 1968 took her bay tree with her to prevent the luck being left behind. According to Pliny, "thunder never strikes the laurel", and it "guards the portals of our emperors and pontiffs: there suspended ... before the threshold." The Emperor Tiberius was said to put on a laurel wreath when it thundered, to ward off lightning. Lupton (1579) said laurel would ward off devils and the falling sickness. It was also used as a Yuletide decoration (Aubrey, 1688). Bay trees were thought to wither when the King died (Shakespeare, Richard the Second, II, iv).

It was lucky to bring white heather into the house; but heather of any other colour was unlucky. Some apple trees planted by the Queen Mother are ringed by white heather, because there is an old Highland tradition that anything planted in a circle of heather would be fruitful.

A hydrangea bush planted near the front of the house was said to prevent the daughters of the house getting married. If an ivy growing on the house wall dies, it is said to portend the death of one of the people of the house.

The Fire

Certain woods were not permitted in the fire. It was unlucky to burn apple wood, because it is an ancient symbol of prosperity and plenty. Elder was not burnt, because it would 'raise the devil' or cause a death in the family. Ash was burnt to produce a hot crackling fire:

> "Burn ashwood green
> 'Tis fire for a queen."

In Somerset, hazel twigs were used to make a protective cross in the ashes on the hearth (presumably because it was unlucky to let the fire go out). An oak fire was said to draw off illness from a sick person. Alder trees should not be cut down; this may derive from the fact that they were sacred to Bran. Green cuttings from a tree that had just been pruned should not be burnt, or the plant would never flourish. Holly branches should never be used for sweeping the chimney.

The Dartmoor song gives all the woods and their properties when burnt:

> Oak-logs will warm you well,
> That are old and dry;
> Logs of pine will sweetly smell
> But the sparks will fly.
> Birch-logs will burn too fast,

Chestnut scarce at all;
Hawthorn-logs are good to last -
Catch them in the fall.
Holly-logs will burn like wax,
You may burn them green;
Elm-logs like to smouldering flax,
No flame to be seen.
Beech-logs for winter-time,
Yew-logs as well;
Green elder-logs it is a crime
For any man to sell.
Pear-logs and apple-logs,
They will scent your room,
Cherry-logs across the dogs
Smell like flower of the broom.
Ash-logs, smooth and grey,
Burn them green or old,
Buy up all that come your way -
Worth their weight in gold.

The Orchard

In Yorkshire, a small apple was left beneath the tree as a propitiatory gift, and the tree was thanked for its fruit. Pruning and grafting were done during the waxing moon; hoard apples (those stored for winter) should be picked at the dark of the moon, otherwise the rays would rot them. Holed stones were strung between trees as protective amulets. Once a widespread custom, this was observed at Frogham in Hampshire as recently as the 1950s. In Guernsey the trees were watered with urine to give sweet red apples. Wassailing was a very widespread custom, and a potent fertility rite. In Langport in Somerset, the vicar told Cecil Sharp that it was forbidden to use wooden vessels for Holy Communion. This was probably a survival from interdicts against early local tree cults. The people of the village were at that time still invoking fertility powers for their trees and wassailing them, singing about the wassail cup 'made of the good ashen tree'.

Planting Trees

Various offerings were made when planting trees. In Yorkshire, poplars were planted at lamb-docking time with a docked tail buried beneath them. In Lincolnshire, horseshoes were placed under ash trees (this may have derived from the World Tree, which is an ash tree; the name Yggdrasil means Odin's horse). In Suffolk, gold coins were placed under walnut trees. In Gloucestershire, pieces of coal were buried under perry-pear trees.

The field

In Herefordshire, seedbeds were spiked with rowan and birch crosses on May morning, for protection and fertility. Newly-turned soil was charmed with a hazel stick to keep the faeries away. The charm sign was two crosses with a heart in the centre.

In other areas, a libation of cider was poured on newly-turned soil.

The Harvest

It was also important to use only certain woods in connection with the harvest. The flail, used for threshing the corn, had a handle made of ash, and the swingle (the shorter piece) was made of holly or hawthorn.

> "And then they brought him to a barn
> A prisoner to endure;
> And so they fetched him out again,
> And laid him on the floor.
>
> Then they sent men with holly clubs
> To beat th' flesh from the bones;
> But the miller he served him worse than that
> He ground him 'twixt two stones."
> (from 'John Barleycorn')

In some places, thirteen apple leaves were buried after the harvest to ensure a good crop for the following year.

The Dairy

In the dairies of Westmorland, the churn-staff was made of the Wiggen-Tree (Rowan) to ward off harmful magic which would prevent the butter being made. Similarly milk-pails were made of ash to ward off harmful magic, and stirring poles for cooling troughs were made of hazel to ward off the faeries. In late summer, butter was salted and potted for winter use, but all potting ceased when the leaves of the ash tree fell.

Cattle

Cattle-droving sticks could only be made of certain woods. Willow wood was said to injure the cows. It was unlucky to use elder wood to drive animals to market. Ash was said never to injure the cattle. Hazel and rowan were said to make the cows fatter. To make runaway cows come back, drovers threw holly after them.

In Worcestershire, the Christmas mistletoe was given to the first cow to calve in the New Year. Cattle were said to thrive in a field where a magical hawthorn grew. (A magical hawthorn is a single tree standing alone in a field.) In Sussex, sick cattle were driven under an arched bramble spray to cure illness; or they could be given a curative mash of cider and Good Friday bread.

At Midsummer, rowan and birch were used to protect cattle. Some farmers made passes over their cattle with a lighted branch; others tied rowan twigs to the cows' tails with red thread. Rowan branches were hung on cattle horns and in byres for protection against sorcery. The afterbirth of calves was hung on hawthorn bushes, because hawthorn is noted for its quick and healthy growth, and is often called quickset. This was sympathetic magic to make the calves grow strong and healthy. Similarly, if a lamb died, it was customary to hang it upside-down in a rowan tree, a thorn tree, or other fruit-tree, to protect the others in the flock. In Shropshire, farmers fed the holly and ivy from the Christmas decorations to their cows.

Horses

Various woods were also favoured in connection with horses. Collars of holly and bittersweet were given to horses to protect them from sorcery. Fenland coachmen preferred whips with handles of holly for use after dark. No branch should be cut for whipstock making; it was better to pull up the long shoots around the trunk. Rowan was also used; there was a country saying "If your whipstock's made of rowan, you may ride your horse through any town." Riders also carried an elder twig in their pockets as a charm against saddle-soreness. (It might be worth trying this with bicycles!) At Midsummer, rowan twigs were tucked into horses' bridles to protect them from sorcery. At Hallowe'en, crosses made from rowan were attached to horses' bridles.

Sheep

At lambing time in Yorkshire, hazel catkins were hung around the kitchen fireplace. The hearth has always been sacred; hazel catkins are known as lambs' tails; so this is clearly an act of sympathetic magic to persuade the hearth spirit to protect the lambs.

Pigs

Rowan garlands were used to deflect harmful magic from pigs.

Babies

Protective magic was also used for babies. Pregnant women would kiss an elder tree to bring good fortune for the child. If a pregnant woman eats a quince it is said to make the baby ingenious. An ash fire would be burning on the hearth when the new baby was given its first bath; and in some areas, the first drink given to the baby after it was weaned was ash sap, to protect it from harmful magic. The first nail-parings of newborn babies were buried under ash trees, to make them good singers. To aid teething, a nutmeg was hung on a string round the baby's neck. A good apple crop is said to mean a good year for twins. In Switzerland, a pear tree was planted at the birth of a girl, and an apple tree for a boy. In the Hebrides, birch boughs were placed over the baby's cradle or pram to keep the fairies away.

Illness and Injury

Trees were also used as charms to prevent and cure illness, and to ward off injury. A cross-shaped elder bud was carried as a charm against rheumatism. Acorns were carried to ward off illness and ensure a long life. It was believed that standing under a hawthorn tree during a storm would protect one from being struck by lightning. To get rid of a fever, people pinned a lock of their hair to an aspen tree, and said "Aspen tree, aspen tree, I pray thee / To shake and shiver instead of me." Catching a falling oak leaf is said to ensure that you will get no colds all winter. Walnuts were carried to strengthen the heart and ward off rheumatic pains; walnut leaves were worn on the hat to prevent sunstroke. Rowan berries and/or bark were carried to aid recovery from illness. Walking sticks of rowan were used by people roaming the woods and fields at night, to protect them from sorcery.

In "Howard's End" by E. M. Forster, the locals used to stick pigs' teeth into the bark of the old wych-elm; chewing a piece of the bark was said to cure the toothache.

In some parts the custom for getting rid of gout was to place the fingernail parings and leg hairs of the sufferer into a hole bored in an oak tree, stop the hole up again, and smear it with cow dung. In Cheshire, to get rid of warts, they used to rub the warts with bacon, cut a slit in the bark of an ash, and placed the bacon in the slit, the idea being that the warts would disappear from the hand and reappear as knobbly bits on the bark of the ash. At Berkhamsted in Hertfordshire, a lock of the ague-sufferer's hair was pegged into an oak, then the sufferer was wrenched away, leaving both hair and ague with the tree. Bramble arches were also used for healing people; the method was to crawl backwards and then forwards through the arch three times, preferably from east to west. A traditional charm for healing burns was to float nine bramble leaves in a holy well, then draw them over the burn, saying:

"Three angels came from out the east,
One brought fire and two brought frost,
Out fire, and in frost,
Out fire, and in frost."

In England children were passed through clefts in ash-trees as a cure for rupture or rickets. Thereafter the life of the patient depends on the life of the tree, and if the tree is cut down, the rupture will return and the patient will die. In some parts the method employed was to split a young ash sapling longitudinally and to pass the child three times through the fissure (often at sunrise), then to bind the cleft up again and plaster it over with mud and clay. As the tree healed, so would the child. The whole process symbolised rebirth and a state of wholeness. Willow, holly, and hazel saplings were also used for this. A cure for a nosebleed (Aubrey, 1696) was to cut a chip from an ash sapling up to three years of age at the time of the Sun's entry into Taurus. A cure for ague was to ask a grafter to cut the maiden branch of a young ash tree, which he did as you were on your way home. No money must be paid for this, or it would not work. In Bere Forest, Hampshire, a cure for whooping cough was to drink new milk from a cup made of the wood of the variegated holly. In Shropshire and Herefordshire, feeding the child from a bowl made from ivy-wood was held to cure whooping cough.

A Fenland charm against ague was to scratch the legs with a holly bough (Porter, 1969). A cure for fever was to poke elder twigs into the ground, making sure to remain completely silent. A cure for toothache was to chew on an elder twig, and then poke it into a wall, saying, "Depart thou evil spirit". Toothache was supposed to be caused by an evil spirit, and spirits were supposed to be attracted to elder trees. A cure for warts was to rub them with a green elder twig or an elder leaf, and bury it in the mud; as the twig or leaf rotted, the warts would drop off. Warts and styes could also be got rid of by piercing them with a gooseberry thorn. In Ireland, this was done through a wedding ring.

General Popular Superstitions

"Touch wood": This is generally said after saying something which you do not want to happen, or when wishing for a favourable state of affairs to continue. When Mr. Asquith, in 1915, referred in his House of Commons speech to the insignificant numbers of British war dead, the First Lord of the Admiralty leant forward and touched the Clerk's table. Similarly, when we say that nothing unfavourable has happened to us, we touch wood to avert misfortune in the future. This probably derives from a pagan custom of touching a tree for luck.

Wooden leg: It was considered very lucky to see a man with a wooden leg as you left your house in the morning, but the luck was cancelled out if you looked back at him. It was also unlucky to see the back of a wooden leg before seeing the front. In London, however, it was believed that seeing the back of a wooden leg portended a surprise to come.

A crooked stick: This was placed in the flue of the chimney when boiling "pig's puddings" (black puddings?) to prevent them from bursting. If they did burst, it was because the stick was not crooked enough (Burne, 1883).

Bees on dead wood: If bees swarm on dead or rotten wood, or near the ground, it is said to portend a death in the family.

Champagne cork: A custom still prevalent is to keep the cork from a champagne bottle with the wire 'cage' still twisted around it, and a coin pushed into a slit in the end. This was formerly a sixpence, then an old five-pence piece; now that all the old money has been withdrawn, I have had to make do with the new five-pence pieces. According to Terence Rattigan's mother, you had to keep it until the next bottle of champagne; in other versions, you had to keep it for the rest of your life. Presumably it was considered to keep you in the happy state which occasioned the champagne being broached (birth, 21st birthday, marriage) and to be generally lucky.

Cork as a cure for cramp: A cork placed under the pillow or sliced into discs and worn as an amulet was said to be a cure for cramp.

Birch trees: In Hampshire, it was customary to cross your fingers under birch trees, to ward off sorcery.

Blackberries: Many places had a taboo against eating blackberries after Michaelmas (29th September), either because the Devil had spat on them, or passed his club over them, or passed his cloven hoof over them.

> "Oh weans, ho weans, the morn's the fair,
> Ye mana eat the brambles mair,
> This nicht the Deil gangs ower them a'
> Tae touch them wi' his pooshioned paw."

(Rhyme repeated on the eve of Dumfries Rood Fair)

Dog-rose: A plan formed while sitting by a dog-rose in the hedgerow will never come to anything (Gaskell, 1838).

Falling leaves or petals: It is said to be lucky to catch a falling autumn leaf, or a falling spring blossom.

Monkey-puzzle tree: It is held to cause three years' bad luck if you speak whilst passing a monkey-puzzle tree (Araucaria spp.) It is held to be a good tree to plant on the edge of a graveyard, though, as it would confuse the Devil if he tried to watch a burial from it. (Porter, Cambridgeshire, 1969)

New moon: It was held to be unlucky to see the new moon first through the branches of a tree. The bad luck could be averted, however, by taking out a coin, spitting on both sides, and putting it back in your pocket; this must be done immediately.

Murder will out...

A sycamore near Dover is known as the Lone Tree. A soldier at Dover garrison killed another soldier with a staff. As they were alone, he stuck the staff into the ground, saying that his crime would not be discovered until it took root. He served abroad for many years after that, and his crime was not discovered. Then he returned to Dover, and driven by morbid curiosity, went to look at the place and found that his staff had taken root and become a tree. Stricken with terror, he confessed his crime and was hanged.

Folksong

Many folksongs are survivals of ancient Pagan themes; their melodies reflect the style of ancient music, and some may be survivals of ancient songs, handed down through the oral tradition, gradually changing in the process, but retaining the same themes (as is attested by similar songs collected in widely separated locations, all over the British Isles).

The Pagan reverence for sacred trees and for the spirit of the forest is reflected in many of these songs (such as 'Edward' or 'The Two Brothers'). The theme of the renewal of life also recurs. There were many songs associated with the custom of wassailing, which was intended to waken the apple trees after their winter sleep.

The figure of St. George, found in many songs and folk customs, is a continuation of the figure of the divine hero. Many people regard him as a foreign invasion of English folklore. In fact, he embodies the archetype of the Green Man (cf. Green George, Jack-in-the Green, etc.). His tomb is said to have miraculous healing powers. His festival (23rd April) is close to Beltane, and he represents the vegetation spirit returning to life after the apparent death of winter. St. George is also the patron saint of the Order of the Garter, which is linked to the ancient pre-Christian concept of the divine right of kings.

English kings are consistently associated with oak trees. William Rufus was killed near one; Charles I was associated with them by the common people; and Charles II hid in the Boscobel Oak before fleeing to France (a symbolic rebirth of the monarchy). Oak deities (Jupiter, Zeus, etc.) are linked with the concept of kingship.

The world of faery is also found in songs, and tree lore figures prominently in these ballads. One such is 'Thomas the Rhymer':

> True Thomas lay on Huntlie bank;
> A ferlie he spied wi' his e'e;
> And there he spied a lady bright
> Come riding down by the Eildon Tree.

The lady is the Queen of Elfland, who takes him to her own country for seven years. When they reach that land, she offers him an apple from a tree that grows there, but he wisely refuses, knowing that whoever eats of faery food must remain in Elfland forever:

> Syne they came to a garden green,
>   And she pu'd an apple frae a tree:
> Take this for thy wages, true Thomas;
>   It will give thee the tongue that can never lee.'

> 'My tongue is mine ain,' True Thomas said,
>   'A gudely gift ye wad gie to me!
> I neither dought to buy nor sell,
>   At fair or tryst where I may be.

In another version, however, he offers to pluck the fruit for her, but she refuses him:

> O they rade on, and further on,
>   Until they came to a garden tree:
> 'Light down, light down, ye ladie free,
>   Some of that fruit let me pull to thee.'

> 'O no, O no, True Thomas,' she says
>   'That fruit maun not be touched by thee,
> For a' the plagues that are in hell
>   Light on the fruit of this countrie.

English folk heroes

Robin Hood

Robin Hood is the people's hero, representing freedom and defiance of authority. He may have been based on one or several historical individuals, but a myth has gathered around his name which has all the hallmarks of a divine hero. He was supposed to have lived in the 12th or 13th century; the legend became popular in the mid-14th century. W. H. Stevenson describes him as "a medieval myth, sprung from the mists of Teutonic Paganism, garnished by the prolific muses of the English minstrels". Margaret Murray suggested that there was a connection with the witch-cult, as the Somerset witches (in 1664) called their god Robin, and Dame Alice Kyteler (in 1324) worshipped a spirit called Robin Artisson. There may also have been a connection with Robin Goodfellow. Robin Hood plays were closely associated with Morris Dancing and the May Day ceremonies. The ballads lay great emphasis on the idea that Robin was devoted to Our Lady, and treated women with great courtesy on her account. He disliked clergymen and priests in the extreme (possibly due to the corrupt practices of the Church in the Middle Ages), however, and frequently ambushed them.

The mythological Robin Hood is derived from the divine archer figure, whose aim is always true (cf. Shen I, Rudra, Shiva, Rama, Arjuna, Yvain). In some areas, however, local legends of giants have been assimilated to him. A rock in the River Tame near Arden Mill in Cheshire has marks on it which are supposed to be Robin's fingerprints; he was supposed to have stood on top of Werneth Low (where there was formerly a barrow) and hurled the stone towards the Cheshire Plain. At Brown Down near Chard in Somerset, there are two barrows a quarter of a mile apart, with shallow depressions on the top; Robin Hood and Little John are supposed to have stood on top of these playing quoits, and the shallow depressions are said to have been caused by the falling quoits. Near Halifax, there is a stone weighing several tons, which is called Robin Hood's Penistone. It stands in the corner of Sleight's Pasture, on the road from Nettlepot to Wemmergill. Robin was supposed to have picked it up on the top of a hill called Shacklesborough, balanced it on his right foot, swung it backwards and forwards a couple of times, and then kicked it towards Lunesdale. It broke as it flew through the air, and part fell in Kelton, part in Sleight's Pasture. Another heavy rock in the same district was supposed to have been flung off his spade while he was digging on a nearby hill. Many prehistoric barrows are known as Robin Hood's Butts, supposed to have been used by him for archery practice. Similarly, two stone-lows in Yorkshire, on the road from Hathersage to Grindleford, are known as Robin Hood's Pricks.

There is also a wind in north-east Cheshire and Yorkshire called Robin Hood's Wind. It is "the bitterly cold wind that ushers in the thaw after a long hard frost... said to have been the one discomfort which, for all his hardihood, Robin Hood could not stand." (Christina Hole). It is possible that this represents a link with Woden, the wind god.

Maid Marian

The historical person who was supposed to have been Maid Marian was Matilda Fitzwalter. She had refused to marry King John, so he confiscated her father's land. On going into the forest with Robin Hood, she is supposed to have adopted the name Maid Marian "to show that she is leading a spotless maiden life" until his outlawry is over and he can marry her. After his death, she retired to Little Dunmow priory, where she was poisoned by King John. There is no real evidence that Matilda Fitzwalter was connected with Robin Hood, but because of the manner of her death, she was regarded as an English heroine who had defied the Norman tyrant, so it was quite natural to link her name with Robin Hood. She was an important character in the May Games. In some places the May Queen was called Maid Marian. This may precede the tradition of her being Robin's wife, as the May Queen is connected with Flora, the Roman goddess of spring. The earliest written reference to Marian as Robin's wife is in "The Ship of Fools" (1500).

The Merrie Men

The other outlaws were attached to the legend gradually. The earliest mentioned companion was Little John in 1341. Robin was supposed to test new recruits by fighting with them. If they were strong and brave, they could join the outlaw band. Friar Tuck and George a Green, the pinner of Wakefield, were enrolled in this manner. The companions mentioned in the Lytell Geste are Gilbert of the White Hand, Much the Miller's Son, and Will Scathelock (or Scadlock, later Scarlet). Will Scarlet joined the outlaws after the girl he wanted to marry was snatched from the church door by Robin (she was being made to marry someone else against her will) and the couple were married in the greenwood.

Robin Goodfellow

The faery known as Robin Goodfellow was closely associated in the popular imagination with the Devil. Robin may have been related to the horned god. A tract of 1638 shows Robin Goodfellow dancing on goat's feet in the midst of a circle of witches. He is mentioned in an old charm against evil spirits. According to Keightley in "Fairy Mythology", he was also called Robin Hood. Shakespeare's portrayal of Puck in "A Midsummer Night's Dream" derives most of its attributes from Robin Goodfellow.

Puck

In Ireland there is a spirit called the Pookah, Phooka, or Pooka, which is a wild shaggy colt hung with chains, which haunts wild places. In Wales there is the Pwca, who likes a nightly bowl of milk, and leads travellers astray in the night. In Kipling's "Puck of Pook's Hill", Puck is portrayed as the first faery to arrive in Britain, and the last one left. He lives in a hill in the Sussex Weald, where he has watched deities, heroes, and invaders come and go.

St. George

The historical St. George had no connection with Britain other than being its patron saint, but his legend outstripped all other saints in popularity. This is probably because he was assimilated to Pagan hero-myths of dragon-slayers (e.g. Perseus, Siegfried, Sigurd), and made the chief figure in the death and resurrection dramas of the Spring festival. The tales of his miraculous escape from death and his revival by St. Michael made him eminently suitable for this role. All attempts to kill him, however thorough and unpleasant, failed; he kept being resurrected. The day of his martyrdom was supposed to have been 23rd April. The historical St. George was a martyr in the Diocletian persecutions of the early fourth century.

In Islamic legend, St. George appears as Ghergis or El Khoudi. Near Sarafend there was a tomb, supposed to be that of El Khoudi, which was empty. This was because, according to the locals, he has never died, but flies round the world, occasionally revealing himself to mortals.

St. George and the Dragon

In "The Prologue to the Passion of St. George" (12th c.), the dragon was overcome by the sign of the Cross and led back to the city by a strand of the princess's hair. The better-known version appears in "The Golden Legend" by Jacques de la Voragine. The Princess of Silene in Lybia is chosen by lot to be fed to the dragon, and is left by the lake near its lair. There St. George finds her and prepares to defend her. The dragon appears, and the saint asks for God's help, fights fiercely with the dragon, and overcomes it. Then he ties the Princess's girdle round its body, and she leads it in triumph back to Silene. The people of the city, seeing the dragon outside are terrified, until they see that it has been subdued. After converting them all to Christianity, St. George cuts off the dragon's head. Here the tale has been manipulated to identify the dragon with Paganism.

On a psychological level, the myth represents the psyche's struggle to integrate the archetypes. St. George is the Animus, the Princess is the Anima, and the Dragon is the Shadow. The later versions, where the Dragon is killed, represent a failure to come to terms with the Shadow. The version where the Dragon is led by a strand of the Princess's hair is much more satisfactory; if the Shadow is repressed, it will become an even bigger monster.

St. George is one of a long line of slayers of monsters and dragons. Frequently the dragon represents chaos, and must be slain to restore order. Tiamat, the Great Dragon of Sumerian myth, threatened to destroy the world she had created and kill all her children, so Marduk slew her and formed heaven and earth from her body. In the Indian myth, Indra slew the serpent Ahi to get rain for the parched world. The princess is not always rescued by the hero; sometimes she assists him, as Ariadne did by giving Theseus the ball of string.

Culture	Hero	Dragon / Monster	Princess
Sumerian	Marduk	Tiamat (dragon goddess)	-
Greek	Perseus	Sea monster	Andromeda
Greek	Hercules	Lernean Hydra	-
Greek	Theseus	Minotaur	Ariadne
Indian	Indra	Ahi	-
Persian	Mithra	Ahriman	-
Persian	Thraetana	Darak	-
Germanic	Sigurd	Fafnir (serpent)	-
Germanic	Siegfried	treasure-guarding monster	-

Germanic	Gull-Thorir	winged & scaled dragon	-
Germanic	Grettir	Karr the Old (vampire)	-
Anglo-Saxon	Beowulf	Grendel	-
English (14th c., Co. Durham)	Lambton heir	Laidly Worm	-
English (Cheshire)	Thomas Venables	man-eating dragon	-
French (Rouen)	St. Romanus	dragon	-
French	St. Martha	The Tarasque of the Rhone	-
French	St. Martial	a dragon in Bordeaux	-

In some folk tales, the Laidly Worm is a boy or a girl who has been turned into a serpent by a jealous stepmother (this happens in "The Laidley Worm of Spindleston Heughs" and "The Lailly Worm"), and is released from the enchantment at the end of the story. In "Assipattle and the Mester Stoorworm", Assipattle is the youngest of seven sons, who, despite being despised by all his family except his sister, kills the dragon by sailing into its gullet in a little boat, running down into its stomach with a lump of burning peat, setting fire to the oil in its liver, and escaping just in time to watch it burn up and disintegrate. Its tongue was flung up to the moon, fell back to earth, and gouged out the sea which divides Denmark from Norway. Its teeth were scattered all over the place, and became the Orkneys, the Shetlands, and the Faroe Islands. The body coiled into a huge lump, which became Iceland, but continued to burn, which is why there are still volcanoes there. Assipattle also stole his father's magic horse, which was controlled by a blast through the wind-pipe of a goose. There are certain similarities with Odin (magic horse, goose), but also with the legend of Marduk, who forms heaven and earth out of the body of Tiamat, the great dragon.

There were many appearances of St. George in battles. During the Crusaders' attack on Jerusalem, he was seen in a blaze of light on the city walls, leading the army in the assault. During the battle of Antioch, the Crusaders were about to be annihilated by the Saracens when they saw a mighty host led by St. George and St. Demetrius charging down the hillside to come to their aid. St. George was also said to have appeared in the sky over the English army at Agincourt. He was regarded as the symbol and figurehead of Christian chivalry, and various orders of knighthood and social and religious guilds were dedicated to him.

In the 15th and 16th centuries in Leicester, there was a pageant called the Riding of the George. The procession included St. George and the dragon (the Chamberlain's accounts for 1536 show four shillings paid for dressing the dragon). From the 14th to the early 16th centuries, there was a similar event in Norwich. The procession featured St. George; the princess was replaced by St. Margaret (who saw the devil in the form of a dragon). After the Reformation (1552), the saints disappeared, but the dragon was kept on "for pastime". It was popularly referred to as "Old Snap", and was accompanied by "whifflers", who juggled with swords, and men in motley. The Mumming Plays featuring St. George appear to derive from ancient vegetation rites. The saint often fights a Turkish Knight or other adversary.

St. Oswald

This saint was a King of Northumbria. He was killed in a battle with Penda (the Pagan King of Mercia) on 5th August 642 CE. There are two wells dedicated to St. Oswald. One is at Winwick in Lancashire, the other is at Oswestry in Shropshire. The Shropshire one is both a healing and a wishing well, and is used for divination. At the back of the well is a stone which used to be surmounted by a carved head wearing a crown; St. Oswald's head is supposed to be buried there. This is interesting because it closely resembles the oracular head of Mimir, a giant killed in battle in Norse legend. Mimir's head was kept in a well near Yggdrasil, the world tree. St. Oswald's well is amongst trees.

St. Edmund

The saint-king was killed by Danish invaders, and his head was thrown into a thicket at Eglesdene. A group of Saxons searching for the head entered the forest in fear and trepidation. The story of the miraculous preservation of the head and its continued power of speech calls to mind the Celtic cult of the sacred head, as well as the oracular head of Mimir and the head of Bran which was kept in the White Tower in London.

"Then they all went together into the woods, looking everywhere among bushes and brambles to see if they could find the head. And, wonder of wonders, God in his wisdom sent a wolf to watch over the head, and protect it against other wild beasts day and night. The men went about searching, and constantly calling out to one another, as is the custom of woodsmen, 'Where art thou now, my companion?' And the head answered them, saying, 'Here, here, here.' Every time they called the head spoke back to them. There lay the grey wolf watching over the head, with it clasped between his two forepaws. He was greedy and hungry, yet for the sake of God he dared not eat the head but preserved it from other creatures. Then were the men amazed at the wolf's guardianship, and took the holy head away with them, thanking the Almighty for the miracle. And the wolf followed them as they bore away the head, until they came to the town, just as if he were tame, and then returned to the forest."

When they arrived at Beodricsworth (now Bury St. Edmunds), the head and body were placed on a bier. The next morning they had been miraculously joined back together. St. Edmund was subsequently associated with marriage and fertility customs. Until the Reformation, a ceremony called the Oblation of the White Bull was carried out every year by the people of Bury St. Edmunds. The bull set aside for the ceremony was not to be used for ordinary farm work or bull baiting, but allowed to roam in the fields in peace and plenty until it was needed. When a married woman desired a child, the bull was adorned with garlands and ribbons and led through the streets to the main gate of the monastery. The woman walked beside it, stroking its sides and dewlaps. Once at the monastery, the bull was left outside, and the woman went to make vows at the shrine of St. Edmund, and to kiss the flagstones there.

This reverence for a murdered king is not surprising, given the tenacity of the belief in the divine nature of kings. Henry VI, Edward the Martyr, and even Charles I had miraculous cures attributed to them.

Well-dressing

This custom probably dates from pre-Roman times, when wells and springs were held to be the dwelling-places of goddesses. Springs with curative powers due to their mineral-laden waters were particularly revered. When Christianity supplanted paganism, the patronage of these waters was nominally transferred to Christian saints, and the custom of tying rags to the trees surrounding the well survived, eventually developing into the elaborate dressing of wells with floral displays, a custom which flourishes in Derbyshire. The patronage of the Buxton waters was transferred from the goddess Arnemetia to St. Anne. Attempts to abolish the custom by 17th century Puritans and other reformers were resisted. In many places well-dressing was revived in the early Victorian period.

Chapter 3

The Mysteries of the Forest

The tree many-rooted
That swells to the sky
With frondage red-fruited,
The life-tree am I;
In the buds of your lives is the sap of my leaves: ye
shall live and not die.

(from "Hertha" by A. C. Swinburne)

The mythology of various cultures included legends of trees, groves, forests, gardens, and tree spirits and deities. In West Africa trees are revered as the place where the spirits of the ancestors make their dwelling. Trees are revered in all cultures for one reason or another. The tree is the tree of life, the phallus in the womb-garden. The garden is the place of birth (Buddha, Dionysos), and of meditation (Buddha, Jesus). The sacred grove is the archetypal place of worship. There are several archetypes associated with the forest: the woodcutter (e.g. Esus, Gilgamesh); the archer (e.g. Shen I the Excellent Archer, Rama, Nodens, Robin Hood, Yvain, Cupid, Eros, Nimrod); the Lord of the Animals (e.g. Herne, Khumbaba, Rudra); the hermit (found everywhere from Buddhist and Hindu holy men to Christian monks); the Lady of Flowers (Flora, Blodeuwedd, Maid Marian); and the Dying God or vegetation spirit (e.g. Attis, Adonis, Bacchus, Christ, Dionysos, Dumuzi, Hippolytus, Osiris, Tammuz, Virbius) who is the consort of the Great Mother.

The mystery of the woodcutter may be explained by the words of Vishnu: "The seed of all woe, as well as the source of all wisdom, is hidden in this secret. Like an axe it strikes at the root of the tree of worldly vanity." Here the tree symbolises the source of illusion, which must be severed at the root for understanding to be brought about. The secret to which Vishnu is referring is his knowledge that an army of ants seen walking across the floor of the palace may contain ants who are reincarnations of great souls, who have declined from the heights of spiritual evolution and have become entangled once more in maya (illusion), so have been reincarnated as a lower life-form in order to begin again. It is not known whether this was the construction that the Sumerians put on the story of Gilgamesh felling the great cedar, or that the Celts put on the image of Esus, but it is not impossible, since some of the other archetypes associated with the forest are common to most of the Indo-European cultures.

The archer is the divine hunter, whose arrows penetrate to the heart of things. Shen I the Excellent Archer is a hero in Chinese myth, which tells that the sun is a raven. At one time there were ten suns, one for each hour of the day. One day, all ten suns appeared in the sky at the same time, threatening to scorch the earth. Shen I the Excellent Archer shot down the extra suns, and found his arrows stuck in nine stones at the top of a mountain. The Celtic god Nodens was a divine hunter and also a river god. In Hindu myth, Rama is an exiled king who takes refuge in the forest, and excels at archery.

The legend of Robin Hood is that he was tricked out of becoming the Earl of Huntingdon, so retreated to the forest. In a French epic poem, the hero Yvain flees into the forest, where he uses the bow for hunting. Cupid and Eros are archers of a different kind, but may well stem from the same archetype; their arrows kindle love. (Curiously, there is a custom among the Bushmen of the Kalahari of a man firing a small arrow from a miniature bow into the buttock of the woman he loves.)

The hunter Nimrod (in Hebrew myth) was 'a mighty hunter before the Lord' (Genesis 10:9). The arrow was also used for divination. Towns were founded by firing an arrow to see where to start building. Robin Hood was supposed to have chosen his hideout at Robin Hood's bay (about 6 miles from Whitby) by firing an arrow from the top of a hill called Stoupe Brow Beacon. He also fired an arrow as he was dying, and told Little John to bury him where the arrow was found. The twang of the bow-string is held to have magical properties, and some hunter-gatherer peoples use the bow as a musical instrument; in fact, the bow is the prototype of the harp.

The Lord of the Animals is a very ancient archetype, representing the most primitive form of consciousness. In India he is Rudra, a god of the dead, a formidable archer who dwells in the mountains, and Lord of all animals (Pasupati). His consort is Prisni, goddess of the dark season. In the Epic of Gilgamesh he appears as Khumbaba, the giant who lives on Cedar Mountain. He appears in the Mabinogion as a black giant of formidable aspect who dwells in the depths of the forest. He is also traditionally the leader of the Wild Hunt. By medieval times he had declined into the despised figure of the Wild Man, but could still command the animals (see section on the forest in medieval literature).

The hermit is the holy man who retreats into the forest to lead a life of contemplation. Buddha did this for a time, and so did his followers; various Hindu sadhus, Christian saints, and other holy men did likewise. The holy man may be wise, or he may be a holy fool. The origins of this probably lie in the shamanic practice of going to the forest to commune with the spirits.

The Lady of Flowers is the young goddess of springtime, embodied by Flora, Blodeuwedd, and Maid Marian. She is a personification of fecundity and the joyful spirit of May. She may have her dark side; Blodeuwedd plots with her lover

Gronw to kill Llew Llaw Gyffes; Maid Marian has been identified in some versions of the Robin legend with the Abbess of Kirklees, who bleeds Robin Hood to death.

The Dying God is found in every Indo-European culture in one guise or another. He is the consort of the Great Mother, and springs from the tree only to be killed as a sacrifice, whether to redeem his people or to bring enlightenment. He is the vegetation spirit, which dies every year and is reborn in spring.

The Great Mother appears in many legends; she is Cybele, Aphrodite, the Virgin Mary, Inanna, Venus, Isis, Ishtar. Her role in these legends is usually that of the great goddess of Nature; her son and lover is often born at the Winter Solstice, grows to be a man, and is sacrificed on the Tree in his prime. The details of the legend vary, but the Great Mother remains.

The forest itself is a place of mystery, the locus of legend, the place of initiation. Its mysterious twilight can be treacherous, the dwelling of mischievous spirits such as the Pookah, Robin Goodfellow, or the Leshy.

In Druidic legend the sun and the forest are married as male and female, light and darkness.

"O the rising of the sun,
And the running of the deer..."

In Australia, the Aborigines view the forest as the Beyond, the realm of shades, and the place of initiation. In Shamanistic lore, it is the dwelling of the spirits.

THE MYSTERIES OF THE TREE IN INDIA

Hinduism

The world tree in Hinduism is the body of Brahman, the Creator. It is also identified with Prajapati, the mythical ancestor of humanity and the world.

Agni, the fire-god, is born of the tree; fire is seen as the rays of the moon dwelling in the wood, because of the primitive method of producing fire by rubbing two sticks together. The tree is the moon mother. The moon tree is associated in India with Soma; Hindu myth tells us that the Gods drank the Soma of the heavenly tree, thereby gaining immortality. The Hindu women of Maharashtra, whenever the New Moon falls on Somavara (Monday, the moon-day), celebrate the rite of soma-vati, dancing round the sacred fig tree.

The forest is seen in India both as a place of refuge and contemplation, and as the abode of demons. One of these is Rudra, the Lord of the Animals, a deity depicted with antlers on his head. He is a formidable archer, whose arrows despatch humans and animals to the world of the dead. He also has a host of spirits called the Maruts, a host of the dead (similar to the Wild Hunt). This power over life and death mean that he is also invoked as a doctor and veterinary surgeon. He also has the power of life and death over the gods; one day he discovered Prajapati committing incest with his own daughter Ushas (who changed into a gazelle to escape her father). Prajapati begged Rudra to spare him, saying that he would make him Lord of all animals. But Rudra shot him anyway, though he wept to think that his arrow had struck the demiurge. Thereafter Rudra was called Pasupati, Lord of the Animals. (It is possible that this story was added to Rudra's legend to account for him being the Lord of the Animals, the original reason having been forgotten; it seems illogical to call him that if he did not spare Prajapati, which was the condition for him to be given the title.) Rudra is probably the prototype for Shiva. The Maruts and their leader are most active in winter, which is called in India *pitrayanam*, the way of the fathers.

Both Rama and Shiva were divine archers. Rama is exiled from his kingdom through the wiles of his stepmother. He and his wife Sita hide in the forest with Rama's brother Lakshmana. Sita is abducted by the demon king Ravana, so Rama enlists the help of Hanuman, the Monkey God, and a thousand monkeys. They rescue Sita from the demon king, but doubt is cast on her virtue. She is about to commit suttee when the funeral pyre miraculously raises her up, she is reunited with Rama, and they are restored to their kingdom. However, the gossip that Sita has been unfaithful to Rama continues, and she goes into exile in the forest, taking her two sons with her. One day Rama is out hunting in the forest, and is killed by his two sons, who do not recognise him and think that he is someone coming to harm their mother.

Shiva is the owner of a magnificent bow, too heavy for any mortal but Rama or Sita to lift. Shiva is also the divine dancer, whose dance creates and destroys. He rides the bull Nandi, and the waters of Ganges flow from his hair.

There is also the recurring image of the woman and tree in Prakrit and Sanskrit texts. It is known as the Salabhanjia: a pose of a woman pulling down the branch of a tree, carved in stone or wood. This does not represent a tree spirit as such, but the ancient custom (also found in Europe) of connecting the life of a person with the life of a tree. There is also the tradition of Dohada, the fertilisation of trees by pregnant women.

However, Dohada and salabhanjia may not be linked, as in salabhanjia the tree appears to be fertilising the woman, whereas in Dohada it is the other way round. Both however probably derive from an earlier tradition of tree-dwelling spirits (around the second or first centuries BCE).

Buddhism

In India, a tree spirit was called a Yaksa. In Indian legend, it is related that when the Bodhisattva went to bathe in the river Nairanjana, he could not get back onto the bank without the help of a yaksa. In the Mahavamsa it is related that when Sakyamuni wished to go among the Nagas, where a war was imminent, he was accompanied on his journey by the yaksa of the tree Rajayatana in the garden Jatavana, which used its foliage as an umbrella to protect him. (The umbrella is one of the attributes of holy or royal personages in India.) Indian female tree nymphs were called Vrikshakas.

In Buddhist art, the salabhanjia often represents Maya, the mother of Buddha, pulling down the branch of a Sala tree at Lumbini to induce labour, so that she might give birth to the Buddha. This image is probably derived from similar pictures of Hindu goddesses giving birth.

The image probably originated in the plucking of blossoms in springtime for making garlands and performing pujas (personal rituals of purification).

Gautama went to the Bodhi tree and sat on the Immovable Spot (the pivot of heaven and earth), facing east. There the lord of the three temporal powers (Kama or Desire, Mara or Death, and Dharma or Social Duty) appeared to him and tried to tempt him. But he was unmoved by all three, and during the night he attained to the Eye of Transcendent Vision, knowledge of his Life beyond lives, and comprehension of the Law of Dependent Origination, by which all beings arise in mutual dependency. He was now the Awakened One, the

Buddha (from the root budh of the verb bodhati, to awake). The bodhi tree was a fig tree (Ficus religiosa); in Vedic and Upanishad texts, it is the World Tree. The Buddha is also identified with the World Tree.

THE SUMERIANS

Depictions of tree worship in the Sumerian (pre-Babylonian) art of Mesopotamia suggests that the fertility goddess and her consort were symbolically related to trees (compare the myths of Cybele and Attis, Ishtar and Tammuz, etc.). Many Sumerian stone carvings depict trees. A dead or sickly tree was symbolic of the death of the natural world. To begin the magic of resurrection, the king sprinkled a potted shrub or a wilting branch with the Water of Life. This resurrection mirrors that of Inanna after her descent into the underworld to seek for Dumuzi. The death of Dumuzi represents the cycle of death and rebirth in nature, and Inanna's descent into the underworld depicts confrontation with death. The god Enki is the gardener in Dilmun, the celestial Sumerian paradise. His activities were mirrored by the King of Eridu, a city of Sumeria. In Eridu, the Tree of Life was associated with the Waters of Life. The King was the guardian of the sacred water and of the sacred grove. One of his titles was 'nukarribu' or 'the Gardener'. The pool beside the shrine represented Abzu or Apsu, a vast underground sacred sea. The Babylonian kings continued this sacred tradition by planting Gardens of the Gods.

Literature reflects the relationship of trees with the fertility goddess; a missing fragment of the Gilgamesh epic, discovered in 1939-40 by Samuel Kramer, tells of a sacred tree:

"After heaven moved away from earth,
After earth had been separated from heaven,
After the name of mankind had been fixed ...
On that day a tree, a halub tree -
On the bank of the pure Euphrates it had been planted
The Euphrates was its drinking water -
Mightily the south wind plucked at its base,
   tore at its crown;
The Euphrates on its waters carried it off.
A lady walking in fear at the word of An,
Walking in fear at the word of Enlil,
Seized the tree in her hand and brought it to Unug:
'To pure Inanna's holy garden thou shalt bring it'
The lady tended the tree with her hand,
   she let it stand at her foot.
'When at last shall I have a holy throne that I may sit on
   it?' concerning it she said;
'When at last shall I have a holy bed that I may lie on it?'
   concerning it she said.
The tree grew large but she could not use it.
At its base the snake who knows no charm
   had set up for itself a nest,
In its crown the Imdugud bird had placed its young,
In its midst Lilith had built for herself a house.
The ever shouting maid, the rejoicer of all hearts,
The pure Inanna, how she weeps!
In that manner her brother, the hero Gilgamesh,
   stood by her.
Armour weighing as much as fifty minas
   he fastened at his waist.
That which weighed as much as fifty minas,
   he treated like thirty shekels.
His bronze axe, his axe of the road,
His axe of seven talents and seven minas,
   he seized in his hand.
At its base he smote the snake who knows no charm;
In its crown the Imdugud bird took its young,

And brought it to the mountain;
In its midst Lilith destroyed her house,
And escaped to the desert places ...
... The tree, he plucked at its base, he tore at its crown;
The sons of the city who had accompanied him
  cut down its crown
Unto the pure Inanna for her throne he gives it
For her bed he gives it."

There are several interesting things about this text. The tree which grew from the separation of heaven and earth has a serpent at its base and an eagle (the Imdugud bird) at its crown, like many trees of life in Indo-European mythology; the difference here is that Lilith sets up house in the midst of the tree, preventing Inanna from using it for her throne. Another interesting thing is that removing the crown of a tree to allow new growth often revives an ailing tree during a drought - perhaps this is the practical purpose of removing the crown.

The identity of the 'halub' tree is uncertain; it may be a poplar or a willow.

The first adventure of Gilgamesh and Enkidu in the Epic of Gilgamesh is their journey into the forest of cedars to confront the giant Khumbaba. Armed but alone, they went to Cedar Mountain. The cedar forest was protected by the enchantments of Khumbaba, such as the magical gate. When Gilgamesh fells a great cedar, a mysterious sleep overcomes him. Eventually, they track Khumbaba down in the deepest part of the forest. The giant almost kills Gilgamesh with the 'eye of death', and is only subdued with the help of the sun god Shamash and the eight winds. Khumbaba is under the protection of the god Enlil, who has appointed him guardian of the forest. The forest is a mythical realm somewhere on the outer bounds of earth and reality. In the middle of it is the Cedar Mountain. Mountains are traditionally the seat of the gods and the centre of the universe, often surmounted by a sacred tree. N. K. Sandars likens Khumbaba to the Celtic Lord of the Animals.

The god Dumuzi, Inanna's consort, was identified with the cedar:

"My shoulder is the cedar, my breast the cypress,
My [?] is the consecrated cedar,
The cedar, the consecrated of Asshur,
The shade of Dilmun."

"Hero, whose body is shining splendour,
Who in the forest of fragrant cedars is cheered with joy,
Standing in the sanctuary of Abzu, the adorned,
  Purified with the sparkling water."

A hymn of Eridu (c. 3000 BCE) describes the sacred tree and the grove surrounding it:

"In Eridu there is a black kishkanu tree,
Growing in a pure place,
Its appearance is lapis lazuli, erected on the Abzu.
Enki, when walking there, fills Eridu with abundance,
In the foundation of it is the place of the underworld,
In the resting place is the chamber of Nammu.
In its holy temple there is a grove, casting its shadow,
Therein no man can enter
In the midst are Utu and Dumuzi,
In between the river with the two mouths."

(The 'river with two mouths' probably refers to the Tigris and the Euphrates, the two sacred rivers of Mesopotamia.)

Another important aspect of the Sumerian mysteries of the tree is the moon-tree, which is the house of the Great Mother. Another hymn of Eridu describes the moon-tree:

"Its root of white crystal stretched towards the deep.
Its seat was the central place of the earth;
Its foliage was the couch of Ziku, the primeval mother.
Into the heart of the holy house which spreads its shade
   like a forest hath no man entered,
There is [the house of] the mighty mother
   who passes across the sky;
In the midst of it was Tammuz."

The moon tree represents the passing of time, which in earliest times was measured by the phases of the moon. The trunk is the changeless axis of the universe and the growth of the branches is the manifestation of time and space. The goddess of fertility is the tree, her son and lover is the new growth, the fire which springs from the wood. The fertilising power of the moon was seen as fire; this power is hidden in wood or tree, sleeping or latent, and can be drawn out by rubbing, the "primitive" way of producing fire. In India, Agni, the fire god, is seen as hidden in the sacred wood from which he is reborn by the friction of the fire stick.

The Great Mother gives birth to the Dying God or Sacral King, then reabsorbs him in death. The moon tree is sometimes depicted as a pillar or truncated tree, sometimes as a growing tree with the moon in its branches. In Assyro-Babylonian depictions of the moon tree, a winged lion and unicorn attend the tree. The winged lion is the waxing moon, the tree is the full moon, and the unicorn is the waning moon. The truncated tree is the Great Mother; a statue of Attis was tied to a truncated pine at the annual festival of his death and resurrection.

Assyro-Babylonian
Moon Tree

Babylonian
Moon-Tree

THE EGYPTIANS

The central myth of Egypt was that of Isis and Osiris. It symbolised the movements of the Nile, the life-giving waters. Osiris (Ousir in Egyptian) as the vegetation spirit represents the corn, the vine, and the trees. He is also the waters of the Nile rising and falling each year; his struggle with Set is the eternal struggle with the barren desert. He is also the god of the dead (Ousir Khenti Amenti: Osiris Lord of the Westerners).

The earliest primitive form of Ousir was the pillar Djed, originally the trunk of a fir or other conifer, carried into battle as a standard. The coffin in which Osiris had been enclosed by the treachery of Set floated down the Nile and across the sea to the Phoenician kingdom of Byblos, where it came to rest at the base of a tamarisk tree. The tree grew rapidly and enclosed the coffin. The fame of this marvellous tree reached the ears of Malcandre, King of Byblos. He ordered the tree to be cut down to serve as the prop for his palace roof. It gave off a beautiful scent; rumour of this spread rapidly. When Isis heard of it she knew it was caused by Osiris. She went to request the trunk of the tree, and removed the coffin from it. She took Osiris to the swamps of the Delta. It was here that their son Horus was conceived, as Isis hovered over Osiris in the form of a hawk. Then Set discovered the body and cut Osiris into fourteen parts, which were spread over Egypt. Isis managed to reassemble him, apart from the phallus, which had been eaten by a Nile crab. (This is the mysterious wound sustained by the Fisher King in the Grail Legend.)

Many other deities were associated with trees. The Lady of the Sycamore, who gives bread and water to the dead, pictured half-emerging from the tree's foliage, was depicted as various goddesses: Ament, Nut, Hathor, Neith, and Ma'at. The sycamore is on the edge of the desert, at the gates of the world. If the dead person eats of the bread and water, s/he becomes 'a friend of the gods', and must follow them into the beyond, never to return. Another goddess associated with trees was Renpet, who wears a long palm shoot with a curved end on her head-dress; it is the ideogram of her name. Palm leaves represent the passing of time, and Renpet is a deity of time's duration, called the Mistress of Eternity, a goddess of the year, springtime, and youth. Thoth (amongst his other functions and attributes) was the keeper of the divine archives and patron of history. He recorded the succession of Pharaohs, and when the Queen had conceived the future Pharaoh after union with the Lord of the Heavens, wrote his name on the leaves of the sacred tree at Heliopolis. On a long palm shoot, he wrote the number of years of reign allotted by Ra to the Pharaoh. Thoth's principle wife is Seshat, who is sometimes depicted alone in the function of divine archivist, and sometimes accompanies Thoth in this function. Seshat is also the patron goddess of architects, the foundress of temples, who helps the king to determine the axis of a new temple by the aid of the stars.

THE GREEKS

Trees appear frequently in Greek myth, as attributes of deities, as places of shelter and succour, and as transformed people. Their psychotropic properties were also known and used; the priestesses of Apollo chewed bay leaves and inhaled the fumes of burning laurel to induce a prophetic state.

The pomegranate, a symbol of conjugal love and fruitfulness, is an attribute of Hera. It also appears in the legend of Hades and Persephone as the fruit of the underworld. As such, it is an attribute of Persephone. The sacred tree of Hades is the cypress.

The birth of Athene, the owl goddess (who sprang fully-formed from the forehead of Zeus, the oak god, after the hammer of

Hephaestus, the smith god, had cleft a passage for her to emerge), is derived from the lightning blasting the oak, where owls reside.

Athene's own sacred tree is the olive, which owed its fruit to her. Part of the Panathenaea festival involved old men carrying olive branches to the Acropolis.

After the death of Phaethon (the son of Helios who attempted to drive his father's chariot), his sisters, the Heliads, came to weep beside his tomb, and were turned into poplar trees. Their tears became amber which gathered on the banks of the river Eridanus.

Daphne was a nymph transformed into a laurel tree by Gaea to escape from the unwelcome advances of Apollo. The laurel was thereafter sacred to Apollo.

Carya was turned into a walnut tree by Dionysos; hence the nymphs of walnut trees were called caryatids.

When Pan seduced the nymph Pitys, who preferred him to her other suitor, Boreas, the North Wind, the enraged Boreas flung her against a rock, crushing her limbs. Gaea, the earth goddess, turned her into a pine tree.

The story of Philemon and Baucis tells of another transformation. They were poor cottagers in Phrygia, who entertained Zeus and Hermes, who were disguised as travellers, so hospitably that Zeus transformed their cottage into a temple, making them its priest and priestess. They asked that when their time came to die, they might do so together, and it was so. Philemon became an oak, Baucis a linden tree, and their branches intertwined at the top. (The story is related in Ovid's 'Metamorphoses', Book VIII.)

Hera, the Queen of Heaven, was born near a water willow on the river Imbrasos on the island of Samos; hence the willow tree is sacred to her.

During the birth of Apollo and Artemis, their mother Leto 'clasped a palm tree in her arms, pressed the soft ground with her knees, and the earth beneath her smiled and the child leapt into the light.' (Homeric hymn to Apollo.) Apollo's sacred trees are the palm, laurel, olive, and tamarisk. Poets were crowned with laurel because it was sacred to Apollo. Laurel was also sacred to Artemis Agrotera, goddess of forests.

Oak trees were sacred to Zeus. During periods of drought the priest of Lycaean Zeus would touch the fountain of the nymph Hago with an oak branch. At once a mist would arise, become a cloud, and bring rain.

The spirits of oak trees were the Dryads; they were crowned with oak leaves and armed with axes to punish harm done to their trees.

The festival of the Septeria commemorated Apollo's purification after killing the serpent Python. He went to the Vale of Tempe in Thessaly and returned to Delphi crowned with sacred laurel. The Septeria was celebrated every nine years. A youth chosen from the nobility represented Apollo. Accompanied by other young people he would set on fire a hut representing the serpent's lair. Then at the end of the festival the same youths would make a pilgrimage to the Vale of Tempe, practise expiatory rites and return to Delphi with the sacred laurel.

When Hermes stole Apollo's heifers, he put sandals of tamarisk and myrtle on his feet to disguise his scent, and made a fire to cook two of them by rubbing twigs of laurel together.

The union of Zeus and Europa was consummated under a plane tree at Gortyna in Crete; because it witnessed the divine union, the tree was given the privilege of having foliage all year round.

Many deities had their dwelling or their temples in the forest. The temples of Demeter, called Megara, were in the forest. Artemis, the virgin huntress and moon goddess, dwelt in the forest. There she guarded her virginity zealously. One day, as a man called Actaeon was out hunting in the forest, chasing a stag with his hounds, he came to the valley of Gargaphia, near the fountain Parthenius, where Artemis was bathing with her maidens. His senses ravished by her beauty, Actaeon paused to contemplate the goddess, but she saw him. Angry that she had been seen naked by a mortal, she changed him into a stag and set his own pack on him. The hounds tore him to pieces and ate him.

THE ROMANS

It is important, in any study of the Roman religion, to draw a distinction between the ancient religion derived from Etruscan and Italic sources, and the classical Hellenized religion of the later period.

Many Roman deities were imported, but the Romans took them to heart nonetheless. One such was Priapus, who is the protector of orchards, gardens, vineyards, bees, fishing, fields, and flocks. Priapus originated in Mysia, Asia Minor, where he was the local version of Pan. His statue was placed in orchards and gardens.

The archaic rural deities of Rome had a lot to do with trees. Flora was the goddess of fruit trees, the vine, and flowers, but later she became associated with fecundity in general, and her festival became a holiday for the prostitutes of Rome. Pomona was the goddess of fruit trees. Silvanus was the forest god, the son of a shepherd of Sybaris and a she-goat; later he became the god of arboriculture, herds, and the tilling of the soil. At the birth of a child three men struck the threshold with an axe, pestle, and broom (symbolic of civilisation) to keep out the wilder spirits of the fields, of whom the chief was Silvanus. A clear distinction is drawn here between cultivated and wild land. Vertumnus, who successfully courted Pomona, was the god of the changing year and the seasons. His name is probably derived from the verb uorti, to change. In the writings of Propertius, he is presented as the agent of change:

"It is for me that the first bunches of grapes turn blue, and for me the ear of grain swells with a milky juice. Here you may see the sweet cherries, the autumnal plums, the mulberries blushing under the summer sun; hither, crowned with fruits, the grafter comes to discharge his vow - those fruits which the pear tree has borne in spite of itself..."
(Propertius, 4.2.13-18)

The cult of Faunus was essentially a rustic element of archaic Roman religion. An attempt was made in 196 BCE to introduce the cult into urban life by establishing a temple in Rome, but it failed. The urban festival was held on 13th February. The rural festival of 5th December, however, was a lively affair, described in the 'Odes' of Horace. It consisted of dancing in the fields, making an offering of wine and a goat kid to the god on a smoking altar of earth. It expressed the true ancient spirit of Roman religion: "an appeal to the vague and possibly dangerous spirit that guards the flocks to be present, but not to linger too long". Faunus was essentially the spirit of the wild woodland. (The name is probably derived from 'favere' and means 'the kindly one'.) His father was Picus (the woodpecker), one of the sons of Saturn, and his mother was Canente, who died of grief when Picus was transformed into a woodpecker. Faunus was also the father or husband of Fauna, goddess of Earth and fields, also invoked under the name Bona Dea (the Good Goddess). He protected woods, fields, and shepherds, and was worshipped in sacred groves, where he gave oracles, mostly during sleep, or by causing voices to be heard in the countryside. He was also said to have been a lawgiver and one of the first kings of Latium. His attribute is the shawm or rustic pipe, which he is said to have invented. His sacred tree was the bay laurel (Laurus nobilis), which was also sacred to Silvanus, Apollo, Ceres, Eros, and Aesculapius.

The fig tree was sacred to Mercury. The first fig gathered from a fig tree dedicated to the god was called a Mercury fig; eventually the name came to denote first fruits in general. If carving a statue of Mercury, however, the proper wood to use was box.

There was a sacred grove at Tiora Matiene in the Appenines, where there was an oracle of Mars, said to be of great age, where a woodpecker perched on a wooden pillar gave oracles.

When the Romans invaded Britain, Mars was syncretised with various Celtic deities. One of his titles was Mars Rigonemetis, king of the sacred grove. He was compared to Alator, Barrex (or Barrecis), Belatucadros, Braciaca, Camulos (the deity of Camulodunum, now Colchester in Essex), Condate, Corotiacus, Lenumius, Lenus, Medocius, Mullo, Olludios, Ocelus Vellaunus, Rigisamus, Teutates, and Thincsus.

Jupiter was the oak and thunder god. He took on many of the attributes of Zeus at a fairly early date, but he had always been the god of thunder, lightning, tempest, wind, and rain.

The King of the Wood at Nemi was a priest-king of the cult of Diana. On the northern shore of the lake of Nemi was the sacred grove and sanctuary of Diana Nemorensis, or Diana of the Wood. A candidate for the priesthood of this grove could only come to office by slaying his predecessor, so every incumbent stood beneath the most sacred tree of the sanctuary with drawn sword, awaiting his assailant. Only runaway slaves were eligible, and before attacking the current King of the Wood, they had to break off a branch from the most sacred tree of the sanctuary. The annual festival of Diana was on 13th August; women whose prayers she had answered came to the grove wearing wreaths and bearing lighted torches to fulfil their vows. The nymph Egeria and the god Virbius were also worshipped in the grove at Nemi. Virbius was a young mortal under the protection of Diana, who was the Latin counterpart of Hippolytus, a young man under the protection of Artemis. Both were a type of Adonis figure, who were killed because of their love for the goddess (similar also to Attis, Tammuz, and Dumuzi). Hippolytus was dragged to his death by the horses of his chariot, who were menaced by a bull sent by Poseidon. He was christianised as St. Hippolytus, whose feast day was 13th August. The death of the priest-king represented the death of this Dying God figure; its purpose (lost in the mists of antiquity) was the renewal of fertility.

The Romans also used a form of divination derived from trees. This was called botanomancy, and took three forms:

(i) Writing sentences on leaves, which are then exposed to the wind. The answer is gathered from those which are left.

(ii) Interpreting the sounds made by the crackling of leaves burning in a fire.

(iii) Interpreting the sound of leaves crackling when crushed in the hands.

THE CELTS

The most obvious manifestation of the Celtic peoples' reverence for trees is in the Ogham script. However, this has been dealt with elsewhere in great detail, so a brief overview will suffice here. There are other, more ancient, ways in which trees have influenced Celtic myth and legend, and they are closely bound up with the magical practices of the Celts, which were in use until comparatively recently. The importance of the Ogham script for the Celts has been somewhat exaggerated in modern occultism, following its appropriation by Welsh nationalists and other nineteenth century eccentrics keen to discover a mystical Celtic heritage.

There is not much evidence that Ogham was used for divination; it was used, however, for funerary inscriptions. Clearly, with the Celtic cult of the head and the veneration of dead heroes, funerary inscriptions would have had more magical importance than they do today, but even so, the bulk of Celtic magical lore was orally transmitted, perhaps because it was too sacred to be written down. Most of the Celts, apart from the priesthood, were probably illiterate; it is only in our literate society that we rely on the written word as a means of transmitting information; hence the Ogham script is given more importance than it would have had amongst the Iron Age Celts. However, the Ogham script can legitimately be considered magical, since it has been used for that purpose for quite a long time, provided that these things are borne in mind. The important thing in the continuation of a tradition is not mere re-enactment of what it was like in the past (which is not necessarily relevant to the present day) but continuing to develop the tradition in the spirit in which it was begun.

Spurious claims for the antiquity of a magical system, however, do not help this process, but hinder it by chaining its adherents to mere re-enactment of the past. Let us then consider the Ogham as the outcome of a long process, beginning with Ogmios (or whatever inspired person or persons invented the script) which included the nineteenth-century Celtic revivalists and continues today with modern bards. But let us not ignore the Celtic myths which fed into this process, nor the sacred trees and groves which the Celts venerated (amongst other features of the landscape, animals, birds, heroes, and sacred objects).

The Ogham script

Legend has it that Ogham was discovered by Ogmios, the Celtic god of writing. Other cultures also attributed the discovery of writing to a deity. Certainly the use of writing brings about changes in consciousness and permits the classification of information in a new algorithmic way, rather different from the heuristic modes used in a purely oral tradition. This algorithmic consciousness has always been present in humanity, but the invention of writing, as a symbolic means of representing sounds and abstract concepts, permitted the manipulation of information in a new way. We have to some extent lost the heuristic mode in the process, which is regrettable as it may have included some rather interesting mental functions.

The association of the Ogham script with the magical powers of trees gives it a potency all its own, to some extent bridging the gap between the heuristic and algorithmic modes of functioning. The magical powers of the trees are often associated with their physical attributes, handicraft uses, or ritual uses. Where these are known, I have listed them with the symbolic meaning of the tree.

The Oghams are as follows overleaf:

Ogham	Meaning	Tree
Beth	Mother Goddess, purification, renewal (Used in beating the bounds ceremony)	Birch
Luis	Flame; protection against psychic attack (Carried for protection against sorcery)	Rowan
Fearn	Fire; blood; freeing earth from water (Becomes hard when immersed in water; used for piles to support buildings and bridges)	Alder
Saille	Linking; harmony; tides; moon (Willow is used in basketmaking and found near water)	Willow
Nuin	Rebirth; linking upper and lower worlds (In Norse myth the world-tree is an ash)	Ash
Huath	Hag aspect of Goddess; sexuality (Associated with Beltane, the May festival)	Hawthorn
Duir	Door; midsummer; the god Taranis (The oak is used to make doors)	Oak
Tinne	Fire; boldness; fatherhood; unification (Holly was used to make clubs)	Holly
Coll	Wisdom, divination, dowsing (Hazel was used for dowsing and divination)	Hazel
Quert	Eternity, rebirth (Apple is an underworld fruit, eaten at Samhain)	Apple
Muin	Gathering, assimilation, learning (Blackberry pies are baked at Lammas, symbolic of the Dying God, who is reabsorbed into the earth)	Vine/ Bramble

Gort	Scarcity, inadequate harvest	Ivy
Ngetal	Preservation; the written word (The reed was used to make parchment)	Reed
Straif	Strife, punishment, authority (A blackthorn stave was the witch's symbol of authority)	Blackthorn
Ruis	Eternity; sacred to the Crone (Associated with the Underworld)	Elder
Ailm	Rising above adversity; healing; foresight	Elm
Onn	Fertility ("When gorse is in flower, kissing's in fashion" - country saying)	Gorse
Ur	Luck; freshness (Heather is still used as a lucky charm)	Heather
Eadha	Preventer of death; resistance to change	Aspen
Ioh	Last day of the year; rebirth (Often planted in churchyards)	Yew
Ea/Koad	Earth (Ea); the Eight Festivals (Koad)	Aspen
Oir	Childbirth (The spindle is a common attribute of mother goddesses)	Spindle or Gooseberry
Ui/Phagos	Hardness; resistance; solid facts	Beech
Io/ Pethbol	Mystery; the labyrinth; dance	Guelder rose
Ao/Xi/ Mor	The pine: illumination (Ao) Spirit (Xi) The sea (Mor) (The pine was formerly used to make torches)	Pine or Witch hazel

Sacred trees and groves

A common site for venerated trees was on a plain. The top of the tree and the plain were generally described as being equally broad. In early Irish tradition, one of the three sacred trees was the oak, Omna. The sacred tree of Mugna was Eo Mugna, the yew of Mugna. It was said to bear three kinds of fruit, the apple, the acorn, and the nut. (The apple is the fruit of the underworld; the nut is of the earth, representing the child in the womb of the Great Mother; and the acorn is of the sky, the oak being the tree of the sky-god). Also mentioned in early Irish texts are Tortu's tree (an ash), the Tree of Dath-i (an ash), and Eo Rosa (a yew).

Sacred trees were known as Bile, and there was one associated with the Irish Queen Medbh (Shakespeare's Queen Mab) called the Bile Meidbe. These trees could neither be soaked by rain nor destroyed by fire; it was taboo to damage them in any way; and assemblies were held under them (it was a common practice to gather at the local omphalos or nowl for such occasions). The well of Connla was under a sacred hazel tree, whose nuts, falling into the well, fed the sacred salmon swimming there and gave them wisdom. Many votive pits have been found with ash twigs deposited in them, which is significant, as it is regarded as a very powerful tree all over Northern Europe, and especially in the British Isles. The depositing of ash wood seems to have declined during the Roman occupation, however, along with deposits of human bones.

A Celtic sacred grove was called a nemeton by the Romans. The Galatians of Asia Minor met at Drunemeton, the Oak Sanctuary; the Roman name of Nanterre in Gaul was Nemetodurum; there was a Nemeton at Vaison (Vaucluse) in honour of Belesama; there was a Vernemeton (the especially sacred grove) in Nottinghamshire; and Medionemeton (the middle sanctuary) on the Antonine Wall (possibly at

Cairnpapple). These groves probably consisted of a focal point of a sacred tree, frequently also a well or spring, and a shrine to house the sacred objects. Buxton in Derbyshire was called Aquae Arnemetiae, which would seem to indicate the association of a sacred grove with springs, as the name means 'waters of the goddess of the grove'. Celtic groves were frequently replaced by stone temples built on or near the original site by the Romans, who equated many of the Celtic deities with those of their own pantheon, thus creating a syncretised cultus acceptable to the indigenous Celts and the conquerors alike. One such temple was the one near Lydney in the Forest of Dean. Here there are iron ore deposits, first discovered by the ancient Britons, and the Romans continued to work them. Near the iron workings, they built a temple to the Silurian river god, Nodens. The temple was also near the River Severn (Sabrina), and the cult objects recovered from it suggest a connection with the river. Nodens had the role of the divine hunter, so he is likened to Mars, but also to Silvanus. Nodens was also a god of healing (he is associated with thermal springs), childbirth, and dogs. He probably had a common origin with the Irish god Nuada Airgetlam (Nuada of the Silver Hand). Some Celtic deities were successfully "exported", a notable example being Epona, the horse goddess, who was very popular with the Romans. Statues of her were placed in stables.

Tree deities and heroes

Various deities and heroes are associated with trees. One such is known from inscriptions in Gaul, particularly in the Gargonne region, whose name was Erriapus (the local equivalent of Mercury) and who was portrayed as a head emerging from foliage. The god Esus is portrayed on an altar found in the church of Notre Dame in Paris in 1711, wearing a short tunic, bare at the right shoulder, cutting a branch from a willow tree, with another severed branch at his feet. On another face of the stone a bull with three cranes is depicted under the same willow tree. (These cranes or little egrets clean lice from the backs of cattle and perch in willow trees.) The goddesses Arnemetia and Nemetona were deities of the sacred grove. There was also Mars Rigonemetis, King of the Sacred Grove. Boudicca performed rites to her goddess Andraste (Victory) in a sacred grove. The Gaulish god Olloudios, possibly also known in Gloucestershire by the name of Olludios, was portrayed as a genius loci with large projecting ears and deeply sunken dots for eyes, five other similar dots on the body, clawlike feet and hands, and with a spear and a shield. On another altar he is portrayed with a double cornucopia and a hooded tunic, thus giving him fertility as well as martial connotations. A god invoked at Colchester and equated with the Roman Silvanus was known as Callirius (possibly derived from the word coll, hazel). One of the Tuatha de Danann was called MacCuill, son of hazel. The supernatural heroine of an early Irish tale is called Caer Ibormeith, yew berry. In another story, two lovers, Baile and Aillinn, die tragically; from one grave grows a yew tree, from the other an apple tree, and the heads of the lovers appear in the tops of the trees. Lleu Llaw Gyffes, killed by the treachery of Blodeuwedd and her lover Gronw, is transformed into an eagle which perches in a tree. A common literary device was to liken the hero to a great tree. A Scottish Gaelic compliment "Craobh a b' àirde de 'n abhall thu" - "You are the tallest tree in the orchard" illustrates the continuing recognition of the majesty of trees amongst the Celts.

The Lord of the Animals

The god of the forest was also the Lord of the Animals. In the Mabinogion he is described as "a black man of great stature on top of the mound. He is not smaller in size than two men of this world. He has but one foot, and one eye in the middle of his forehead. And he has a club of iron, and it is certain that there are not two men in the world who would not find their burden in that club. And he is not a comely man, but on the contrary he is exceedingly ill-favoured; and he is the woodward of that wood. And thou wilt see a thousand wild animals grazing all around him." In the twelfth century 'Vita Merlini', Merlin becomes the Lord of the Animals; dressed in antlers, he summons an enormous herd of stags and she-goats as a wedding gift for Guendoloena, who is amazed at his affinity with the animals. The name Gwendolen means 'white circle', and in this story Guendoloena appears to be a type of flower maiden. (In modern Welsh, 'gwyn' or 'gwen' means white or blessed, and 'dolen' means a ring, link, loop, or bow.) It is appropriate that the Lady of the Flowers should be the consort of the Lord of the Animals. She represents the growth and burgeoning of nature; he represents the powers of hunting, culling, and death, which must occur so that the powers of fertility can progress without stagnation. Cernunnos is often identified with the Lord of the Animals, since he (or some other antlered god) is depicted on the Gundestrup cauldron with a stag and other animals, and holding a ram-headed serpent in one hand and a torc in the other.

Magical objects

The Gaelic white wand was made of yew; the Celtic wand was made of hazel. Many statues and heads were carved from wood, frequently oak. The Druids' staffs of authority and magical shields were made of hazel. The different qualities inherent in the different kinds of wood were carefully chosen to match the purpose of the object being made, whether "secular" or "religious" (though there was not much distinction between the two, since all aspects of life were imbued with magico-religious significance). See the comments on the uses of trees accompanying the Oghams above.

Conclusion

It is very difficult to piece together a coherent picture of the spiritual life of the Celts; they were not a contemplative people, but rather revelled in their heroic and warlike exploits. However, it is clear that trees, wells, votive pits, the cult of the head, birds, animals, and the veneration of dead heroes played a large part in their religious life. Accurate observation of natural phenomena is a marked characteristic of the Celts. Sacred groves were usually the focus of their rites, and there was a priesthood to act as mediators between the people and the deities. With the coming of the Romans, the picture changed somewhat, with the introduction of new deities, stone temples, more urbane religious forms, and the suppression of the Druids. It is clear, however, from medieval penitentiaries, that the veneration of trees and wells continued well into the Christian era, and has survived or been revived in some places, continuing right up to the present day in one form or another. It must be emphasised that this does not necessarily indicate a survival of paganism per se, but rather a continuation of ancient magical customs into modern times.

THE GERMANIC PEOPLES AND THE ANGLO-SAXONS

The Germanic peoples lived in an area that was covered by vast tracts of forest, so it loomed large in their awareness. The name for a wood or grove in modern German is 'der Hain', which has connotations of sacredness. Germanic folklore abounds with legends of the Wild Hunt (der wilde Jagd, das Totenheer), led by Odin, Berchta, or Holda.

The Wild Hunt rode through the forests, an eerie cavalcade of the souls of the dead, the Blessed Folk. Valkyries and slain heroes were among the Seely Host; geese flew in front of it, their honking echoing the cries of the dead.

The Anglo-Saxon word for Valkyries was waelcyrge, meaning slaughter-choosers. The waelcyrge were associated with the Wild Hunt, and also with bees, spears, thorns, and spindles. Bees were described as weaving the honeycomb, which was called the bee-web. The stings of bees were analogous to spindles and spears. Another name for the waelcyrge was sigewif (victory-women), and bees are addressed as sigewif in the charm 'Wid Ymbe'. The concept of 'elf-shot' is also closely connected with this symbolism; the aim of charms such as 'Wid Faerstice' was to harm an enemy from afar by wounding them with invisible arrows (elf-shot or the spears of the waelcyrge). The art of the healer often consisted in removing elf-shot from the victim.

Anglo-Saxon Magic

Trees were less used than herbs in the magic of the Anglo-Saxons, but many different species of tree were used. The magician would take small pieces of the tree: a leaf, a twig, or a piece of bark. In the charms of the Leechbook and the Lacnunga, the following species are mentioned: elder, ash, oak, blackthorn, elm, trembling poplar, hazel, apple, holly, alder, willow, sallow, myrtle, crab-tree, aspen, thorn, nut-tree, woodbine, maple, birch, hawthorn, black alder, spindle, wych-elm, olive, wild olive, goat-willow, vine, and mistletoe.

The most popular method of using the magical power of the tree was to take a piece of bark, grind it to a powder, and put it into an ointment or drink. The bark was gathered near the base of the tree (Leechbook I, xxxii), near the earth (Leechbook I, xliv), in the earth (Lacnunga 43), on the east side (Lacnunga 12), or on the north side (Leechbook I, liv).

A recipe to cure shingles (OE circul-adl) included bark from the trembling poplar, aspen, apple, maple, elder, willow, sallow, myrtle, wych-elm, oak, blackthorn, birch, olive, and goat willow, plus a lot of ash and "part of every tree one can get except hawthorn and alder", plus various herbs. The mixture was then boiled three times, more herbs were added, with butter, barley meal, burnt salt, and pepper. This was given to the patient after a night's fasting, after which the patient had to drink powdered mistletoe in wine, then avoid various foods and "be moderate in the way of wine and ale" (Leechbook I xxxvi). See Appendix Three for Anglo-Saxon tree names.

Heroes and heroines

The poem "The Waking of Angantyr" recounts the shamanic journey of Hervor, who walks between the worlds seeking supernatural power. She wakes her father in his barrow to obtain secret knowledge. He reveals various secrets and gives her the dwarf sword Tyrfing, a sword that carves unhealable wounds and brings death and misfortune to its bearer. Hervor leaves the realm of the dead, Samsey, exulting in her newfound power, and saying:

> "Vikings, farewell! I'll follow my road,
> and go in haste. Be whole in your grave!
> Now I have walked   between the worlds
> I have seen   the fires circling."

Volund (known in England as Wayland) the smith god was also associated with talismanic weapons, dismemberment, and magic flight. However, Odin was the deity most characteristic of shamanism. Odin is the god of the raging wind, who hung on the World Tree, Yggdrasil, to gain knowledge:

"I know that I hung   on a windswept tree
   for nine whole nights
wounded with a spear   and given to Odinn
   myself to myself
on that tree   which no-one knows
   whither the roots of it run.

None gave me bread,   none gave me drink;
   Down to the depths I peered,
I took up the runes,   screaming I took them;
   Thereupon I fell back."

(The Havamal, stanzas 138-9)

Some historians have suggested that the myth of Odin hanging on the World Tree is derived from the myth of Christ on the Cross. This view is clearly erroneous, since many shamanic cultures included the practice of hanging on trees as a form of initiation, and the sacred grove at Uppsala in Sweden had sacrifices to Odin hanged on the trees. Hanged men in general were regarded as sacrifices to Odin, and the name Yggdrasil means Odin's horse (Ygg being one of his by-names), referring to the way the death-throes of a hanged man resembled someone riding an invisible horse. In the poem "The Dream of the Rood", the Cross of Christ is made to seem as much like a tree as possible, in order to make the legend acceptable to an Anglo-Saxon readership:

"It seemed to me that I saw   a most wondrous tree
Lifted up aloft   with light wound round
   Of trees the brightest."

Indeed, the purpose of Odin's hanging on the tree was quite different from that of the crucifixion of Christ. Christ's purpose was the redemption of humanity from sin. Odin's purpose was to retrieve esoteric knowledge from the depths by undergoing a near-death experience. By hanging on the World Tree, he identifies himself with the universe ("myself a sacrifice to myself") and the microcosm with the macrocosm. The depths of the void become the inner depths of the soul, and the Runes are the mystery which is revealed to him. However, Odin is not only a god of shamanic transformation and death; he is also the giver of life, the divine breath. With Vili and Ve, his two brothers, he created Ask and Embla (the first man and woman) from two tree trunks on the shore by breathing life into them. (This is the mythological source of the rune Os, meaning the divine breath or speech.) He is also closely associated with groves, trees, hills, and political authority. He reconciled the two aspects of life within his own person, embodying both order and chaos. He is the giver of life, but also lord of the gallows and leader of the armies of the dead. He is the lord of the sky and the wind, the trees and the hills, but also the god of tribal worship and family life. He inspires poetry and passionate love, but he also embodies the berserk frenzy of the warrior.

In the Grimnismal, it is related that Odin was suspected of magic, bound, and placed between two fires. But he had a vision of the religious mysteries, the creation, Yggdrasil, the horses of the sun, and the dwellings of the gods, which gave him such strength that he was able to break his bonds and appear in his full divine glory. The name Grimnir means the masked one or the disguised one.

The World Tree is Yggdrasil, the Mighty Ash, the Ever Green, the fountain of life, eternal life, and immortality. The gods meet in council beneath its branches; its roots are in the depths of the underworld. The trunk passes through Middle Earth, and the branches are in the heavens. Hence the tree unites the three worlds. From its roots rises the fountain Hvergelmir, the source of all rivers and of earthly time. The roots are constantly attacked by the dragon Nidhogg, the Dread Biter, representing the malevolent forces of the universe. Odin's horse Sleipnir browses on the leaves. In the boughs the eagle of light and the serpent of darkness are eternally at war. The squirrel Ratatost, a mischief maker, carries insults from one to the other, creating strife between them. In some legends Ratatost has a more constructive role as a messenger between the three worlds. There are four stags in the branches, representing the four winds, which browse on the leaves. The leaves are renewed by the Three Norns or Wyrd Sisters, who water the tree. The solar cock, a symbol of vigilance, is sometimes depicted on the branches. The worlds are linked by the Bifrost or Rainbow Bridge (which connects Midgard and Asgard, and is guarded by the god Heimdall), and a bridge of ice (which connects Midgard and Hel, and is guarded by the goddess Mordgud).

The nine worlds of Yggdrasil are:

Asgard	(abode of the Aesir pantheon)
Lightalfheim	(abode of the Light Elves)
Vanaheim	(abode of the Vanir pantheon)
Midgard	(Middle Earth)
Muspellheim	(realm of fire)
Nifelheim	(realm of fog)
Svartalfheim	(abode of the Dark Elves, or dwarves)
Jotunheim	(abode of the ice giants)
Hel	(realm of the dead)

The Well of Wyrd is in Asgard. The Three Norns dwell there, weaving the fate of humanity. They are Urd (fate), Skuld (being), and Verthandi (necessity).

The Well of Mimir, somewhere in Midgard, contains the oracular head of Mimir, a wise giant killed in battle. The Well of Mimir is also a metaphor for the starry deeps of space and the night.

Asgard was identified by Snorri Sturluson with Troy; he says that Asgard was built "in the centre of the earth"; "at that time it was called Troy." However, the Pole Star (the turning point or Nowl of the heavens) was called Troja, meaning a turning point, so he may have been confusing the two, since Asgard was regarded as being located at the Pole Star. The same etymological confusion occurred later, when mazes, which had been known as Caer Droia (a place of turns), were called Troy Town. Similarly, Britain was identified with Troy; because it was regarded as the last outpost of civilisation, it was also called a turning point, and became confused with Troy.

The Runes, discovered by Odin whilst hanging on the World Tree, are associated with trees; each rune corresponds to a tree with similar symbolism.

Rune		Meaning / symbolism	Tree(s)
Germanic	Anglo-Saxon		
FREYR & FREYJA'S AETT			
Fehu	Feoh	The primal cow; property; good name	Elder
Uruz	Ur	Horns of the ox; strength	Birch
Thurisaz	Thorn	Thorn; Thor's hammer; phallic power	Oak/Thorn
Ansuz	As/Aesc	World Tree; knowledge	Ash
Raido	Rad	Cart; journey	Oak
Kano	Ken	Torch, illumination	Pine
Gebo	Gyfu	Sacred mark; an exchange of gifts	Ash/Elm
Wunjo	Wyn	A wind vane; joy; glory	Ash

HEIMDALL & MORDGUD'S AETT

Rune		Meaning / symbolism	Tree(s)
Hagalaz	Haegl	Hailstone; the beams of a house	Ash/Yew
Nauthiz	Nyd	Fire-bow; need-fire; catharsis	Beech/Rowan
Isa	Is	An icicle; steadfastness; standstill	Alder
Jera	Ger	The cycles of the year	Oak
Eihwaz	Eolh	Yew trunk; the underworld	Yew/Poplar
Perth	Peordh	The womb, birth; the mysteries	Beech/Aspen
Algiz	Elhaz	Elk; flying swan; splayed hand; sedge; protection; cosmic pillar	Service or Yew
Sowelu	Sigel	Rays of the sun; illumination	Juniper/Bay

TYR & ZISU'S AETT

Teiwaz	Tyr	Irmensul; justice	Oak
Berkana	Beorc	Birch; Earth Mother's breasts	Birch
Ehwaz	Eh	Horse; two poles bound; movement	Oak/Ash
Mannaz	Man	Human being	Holly
Laguz	Lagu	Leek; growth; a sea-wave	Osier
Inguz	Ing	Genitalia; fertility	Apple
Othila	Odal	Land; property; inheritance	Hawthorn
Dagaz	Daeg	Dawn; balance of night and day	Spruce

Additional Anglo-Saxon Runes: AETT OF THE AESIR

Ac	Acorn; mark-tree	Oak
Os	Mouth; speech; a river-mouth	Ash
Yr	Yew bow; self-defence	Yew
Ior	Jormungand, the world serpent	Linden/Ivy
Ear	Earth, the grave	Yew
Cweorth	Rising smoke; an offering	Bay/Beech
Calc	A drained chalice; chalk	Maple/Rowan
Stan	Stone; megalith	Blackthorn
Gar	Odin's spear Gungnir	Ash/Spindle

Additional Germanic Runes (not included in any Futhark)

Wolfsangel	Wolf-hook	Yew
Ziu	A lightning-bolt	Oak
Erda	Mother Earth	Elder/Birch
Ul	Turning point; Yule (Midwinter)	Sea Buckthorn
Sol	The Sun Goddess; the sun's disc	Juniper

The Holly King and the Oak King

Baldur was the solar oak god of Germanic mythology. He embodied the spirit of the oak tree. He could not be killed by anything but a dart of mistletoe. Since the life of the tree is believed to reside in the mistletoe, it must be broken off before the tree can be cut down. Similarly, Baldur's life resided in the mistletoe. Norse legend relates that he was troubled by evil dreams and presentiments of death. His mother, the goddess Frigg, begged every being and thing on earth to swear an oath not to harm Baldur. Everything - metal, fire, water, minerals, stones, plants and trees, illnesses, birds, animals, and venomous creatures - gave a solemn promise not to harm him. From then on Baldur was invulnerable, so the gods developed a game of throwing things at him, but he was impervious to all blows.

Loki watched all this and loathed Baldur, who was so beautiful that he shed light around him. So he assumed the form of an old woman, and went to Frigga, asking what the source of the gods' mirth might be. Frigga explained what had happened, and how everything had promised not to harm Baldur. Loki asked if there was anything she had forgotten, and she admitted that she had overlooked one small plant because it had seemed too young to take an oath - the mistletoe. So Loki left the presence of Frigga, resumed his normal shape, and went to gather the mistletoe. Then he returned to Asgard and sought out Hodur, Baldur's blind brother. He asked why he was not joining in the game, and Hodur replied that it was because he was blind. So Loki put the mistletoe in his hand, and guiding his aim, told him to throw it at Baldur. Hodur threw the mistletoe, which pierced Baldur and killed him. All the gods were stricken by Loki's treachery, but could not punish him in the place where they were assembled because it was sacred.

Frigga asked if anyone was willing to descend to Hel to rescue Baldur. Hermod mounted Sleipnir and rode to Hel. The goddess Hel was willing to let Baldur return to Asgard, provided that it was the desire of every being in the universe. Hermod returned to Asgard with this news, and the gods asked all the world to grieve for Baldur. The whole world grieved for him except the giantess Thokk, who was none other than Loki in disguise, so Baldur was obliged to remain in the underworld.

This myth is probably a version of the theme of the twin gods, the dark twin and the light twin, the Holly King and the Oak King. The dark twin (Hodur) is King of the Waning Year, and the light twin (Baldur) is King of the Waxing Year.

Sacred Groves

The only traces of Anglo-Saxon holy places are found in place-names. 'Ealh', meaning temple, occurs only twice, in Kent; 'hearh', meaning a hilltop sanctuary, is found in the Midlands and the south-east; and 'weoh', meaning sacred space, is found over most of the areas settled by the pagan English. Also, the word 'legh' or 'leah' (modern English leigh or lea), meaning a cleared space, is associated in some place-names with Woden and Thor.

It is very difficult to distinguish between temples and domestic buildings; only one temple has been positively identified, at Yeavering in Northumberland, and that had been burnt down. It was evidently a temple because there was no domestic detritus, but there was a pit filled with animal bones, mainly ox skulls, a deposit of which was found at a 'hearh' at Harrow in Sussex. In addition to these signs , the suffix '-ey' appears to indicate a sacred place (e.g. Coveney, near Ely). See Appendix One for place-names reflecting pagan activity and sacred trees.

THE CHRISTIAN AND GNOSTIC MYSTERIES OF THE TREE

The Tree of Life and the Tree of Knowledge grow in Paradise. The Tree of Life is at the centre and signifies regeneration and the return to the state of primordial perfection. In the Garden of Eden myth, God casts Adam and Eve out of the garden lest they eat of the fruit of the Tree of Life, and live forever. The Tree of Knowledge is dualistic, giving the knowledge of good and evil. The Fall of Man was seen as being due to the Tree of Knowledge, and the Redemption by the Tree of the Cross. There is a persistent ophitic tradition (from Greek ophis, a serpent) of Christ depicted as a serpent. There are two sources of this tradition: Christ's words to Nicodemus (John 3:14), likening himself to the serpent of bronze lifted up by Moses in the wilderness (Numbers 21:6-9); and the Gnostic interpretation of the Garden of Eden myth. To the Gnostics, the serpent on the Tree of Knowledge was the first to attempt to release humanity from bondage to an unknowing god (the archon Ignorance) who had identified himself with the Absolute and was blocking the way to the Tree of Life. Therefore Christ was identified with the serpent because he came to bring enlightenment (gnosis).

> "Then the Lord sent venomous snakes among them; they bit the people and many Israelites died. The people came to Moses and said, "We sinned when we spoke against the Lord and against you. Pray that the Lord will take the snakes away from us." So Moses prayed for the people.
>
> The Lord said to Moses, 'Make a snake and put it up on a pole; anyone who is bitten can look at it and live.' So Moses made a bronze snake and put it up on a pole. Then when anyone was bitten by a snake and looked at the bronze snake, he lived.
>
> (Numbers 21:6-9)
>
> "Just as Moses lifted up the snake in the desert, so the Son of Man must be lifted up, that whoever believes in him may have eternal life."
>
> (John 3:14-15)

The serpent coiling round the tree is found in many traditions, and usually represents the life force (Kundalini) or earth energy.

In the writings of some Christian mystics, the cross is identified with the world tree:

> "This wood is provided for my salvation... I establish myself in its roots, I lay myself down under its branches... Its fruit provides me with perfect joy... This tree goes up from the earth into the heavens... it is the plant of immortality, rising in the middle of heaven and earth - the firm prop of the universe, joining all things together."
>
> (St. Hippolytus)

In India there is a belief in Dohada, the fertilisation of trees by pregnant women, which found its way into the Koran with the legend of Mary the mother of Christ sitting under a palm tree which Allah then made fertile, and thence into various songs and legends of Europe.

In medieval art, pictures of the Annunciation of the birth of the Virgin Mary to Anne, her mother, show Anne sitting under a laurel tree. The story was that Anne, seeing a nest of sparrows in the laurel tree, said, 'Woe unto me, even the fowls of the heaven are fruitful', because she was barren. This seems to be a case of the tree fertilising the woman (salabhanjia in Hindu myth).

THE FOREST IN THE MEDIEVAL IMAGINATION

The medieval view of nature in literature and art was symbolic and allegorical; according to Christian belief, the ultimate reality was God, so it behoved the Christian to ignore the beauties of nature and concentrate the mind on God. However, it may have been realised that meditating on nature would lead the mind to the divine, as an inscription on the facade of the abbey church of St. Denis read: "... through sensual beauty the soul is elevated to true beauty, and from earth... it is raised to the heavens... "

The forest represented the wild and untamed part of nature. Human habitation was scattered here and there in the forest, lonely and remote hamlets in clearings and glades. The forest proper was peopled with wild animals, robbers, ghostly beings, and werewolves, and the faeries and the Wild Hunt pursued the unwary traveller. However, the forest was also a source of game, fuel, building materials, fruit, honey, and a place to graze pigs, so it was also beneficial to humans.

Christian saints and hermits in Northern Europe could not seek solitude in deserts like their Mediterranean and Near East counterparts. Some, like St. Brendan, went to sea to find the same kind of experience; others went into the depths of the forest. Their aim was to escape from the sophistication of urban life, to return to the simple life, nature, and solitude.

St. Ronan was an Irish saint who settled in Brittany. According to 'The Life of St. Ronan' (13th c.), "He plunged deep... into the desert and reached the forest of Nemet in Cornwall." It was obviously a Pagan sacred place, since the name appears to be derived from the Roman word for a Celtic sacred grove, 'nemeton'. Working miracles, St. Ronan protected the nearby population from wolves, but aroused the anger of 'Satan', who finally drove him away through the 'diabolical' peasant woman Keban. Clearly he offended the forest god and his priestess. It is interesting that her magic prevailed.

Many hermits lived completely in harmony with the forest. In the forest between Maine and Brittany there lived a young hermit called Pierre. He dwelt in a small house made of bark, and ate young tree shoots, nuts, berries, and honey; "...all these riches seemed to spring from the horn of plenty itself" (from "The Life of St. Bernard of Tiron", by Geoffrey the Fat).

The forests of Europe benefited from a warmer than usual climate in the period 500 - 1200 CE, and enjoyed a period of resurgence. The forest of Ardennes (Arden in Shakespeare's "As You Like It") had been regarded as the archetypal forest since Celtic times, and it was a vast tract of forest.

The first recorded use of the word forest was in a charter granted by Sigebert III to the abbey of Stavelot-Malmedy in 648 CE. "In our vast forest named Ardennes, a vast solitude in which animals reproduce..." The word is derived from the Latin 'silva forestis', a forest under the jurisdiction of a royal tribunal (forum). It passed into some of the European languages (though older words continued to be used as well), becoming *Forst* in German and *forêt* in French.

The Wild Hunt

The Wild Hunt is the cavalcade of the god of the dead and the people of the underworld, which rides through the forest or on the storm. It symbolises death as the necessary complement to life. Death must occur so that new life can take its place; the leaves must fall from the trees in autumn to make way for the new growth in spring.

The dead warriors of Odin's host were called the Herjar. When referred to as the leader of the host, Odin was often given the name Herian, which developed into the names Harilo, Herela, Herleka. This last was Latinised as Herlekinus, which became the Herlequin of French legend, and the Harlequin of the commedia del arte and the French theatre of the 16th to 18th centuries. It could be significant in the light of this that

Harlequin wears a mask. Odin's title "Herian" was probably known in Britain, as in the Old English poem "Widsith", the poet mentions that he sought the Herelingas. This may be a reference to the Herjar as well as the Harlung brothers, who were hanged in the fourth century by their uncle, King Ermanaric of the Goths. As the audience of the poem would have known that hanged men were sacrifices to Odin, they would not have missed the allusion. There is no proof that the name Herian is the origin of Herne, but it is not impossible. Clearly Herne represents the same archetype as Odin, though his legend has arisen from the inner realms of the land of Britain, shaped to a certain extent by the local group mind, but with most of the features of his counterparts in other Indo-European cultures (Rudra, Odin, etc.).

The Wild Hunt sometimes appears with a wagon or cart in the procession. This is probably associated with Charles' Wain (Anglo-Saxon carleswaen), one of the old names for the constellation of the Plough, which is probably a reference to Woden as lord of the sky (carl meaning man), though it was later taken to refer to Charlemagne, who appears as the leader of the Wild Hunt in later folklore.

Originally associated with Odin in Germanic legend and Herne in Anglo-Saxon myth, the Wild Hunt became the entourage of Satan in some medieval stories. The connection was inferred from a reference in Psalms to Satan as a hunter who lays snares to catch the souls of the unwary. "*Quoniam ipse liberavit me de laqueo venantium, et a verbo aspero.*" (For He has freed me from the snare of the hunter, and from harsh words. - Psalm 91.3) This image is developed further in various texts. Hugh of St. Victor wrote that "*Cerva est casta et munda anima. Sagittae sunt desideria mala. Venatores sunt daemones.*" (The hart is the chaste and pure soul. The arrows are evil longings. The hunters are devils.) So the Pagan myth of the Wild Hunt as the divine Hunter and his crew purifying by selection and sacrifice was distorted into the Christian devil hunting down souls. This distortion was brought about by the fear of death induced by belief in hell as a place of torment. Whereas the Pagan view is that souls descend into the Underworld to be renewed, and sees the Lord of the Forest as the guide and psychopomp, the new religion declared that he was the ultimate Adversary, rather than the natural complement to the powers of life.

In the Christian folklore of the Wild Hunt, the dead who rode in the cavalcade were not good enough for heaven and not wicked enough for hell, according to an account from Telemark in southern Norway. They have to ride about until the end of the world, or until all the evil in the world has been righted.

There are two strands in the tradition of the Wild Hunt: a Northern European one, and a Southern European one. Both ultimately derive from the same ancient Indo-European culture. In Northern Europe, the leader of the hunt is Odin or Woden, and Herne. The wild host is called the Totenheer, the army of the dead.

In Southern Europe, the hunt is derived from Hecate and her dogs, the wild hunts of Babylon and Persia, and possibly Rudra and the Maruts in India. On a frieze in the church of St. Zeno at Verona (built 1130 CE), Theodoric appears as the leader of the hunt. An Italian wild host is described by Guicciardini; William of Auvergne records a Spanish one; the Basques have a legend of King Solomon as the leader; in the Tyrol, the leader was called Ourk (Latin orcus).

All over the Eurasian continent, the Wild Hunt is associated with storms, hills, trees, and groves. In Latvia, the Northern Lights are said to indicate that the dead are fighting their battles in the sky. In Ireland, O'Donoghue (sounds a bit like Odin) rises from the waters of a lake on 1st May (Beltane), and visits his realm mounted on a milk-white steed. The boatmen of Killarney call the white-crested waves when the wind whips up the sea "O'Donoghue's white horses". The Wild Hunt was usually seen at night, in winter, and in forests and woods. In India, winter is called the way of the fathers (pitrayanam).

A sighting of the Wild Hunt occurred in 1127 CE, and was recorded in 'The Peterborough Chronicle':

> "Soon after many people heard and saw many hunters hunting. The hunters were huge and black and horrible, and their hounds were black and wide-eyed and horrible, and they rode on black horses and black bucks. This was seen in the said deerfold in the town of Burch, and in all the woods from the same town to Stanford."

Herne the Hunter was also associated with the Wild Hunt. His historical legend (probably introduced when his original meaning was forgotten) was that he was one Richard Horne, Yeoman, who was examined and confessed to poaching. His ghost is said to haunt Windsor Great Park. This story appears in a pirate version of "The Merry Wives of Windsor" produced in 1602. This pirate version was once considered to be Shakespeare's first draft, but it has been demonstrated to have been produced after the real play. However, some writers interpret Herne as meaning 'heron', rather than 'horned'. Since the heron is a hunting bird, however, this need not present a problem, since the waters fished by herons can also represent the Underworld. Shakespeare describes Herne the Hunter as having horns, however:

Mrs. Page: There is an old tale goes that Herne the Hunter,
Sometime a keeper here in Windsor Forest,
Doth all the winter time at still midnight
Walk round about an oak with great ragged horns.
And then he blasts the tree and takes the cattle,
And makes milch kine yield blood, and shakes a chain
In a most hideous and dreadful manner:

You have heard of such a spirit; and well you know
The superstitious idle-headed eld
Received, and did deliver to our age,
This tale of Herne the Hunter for a truth.
Page: Why, yet there want not many that do fear
In deep of night to walk by this Herne's oak:
But what of this?
Mrs. Ford: Marry, this is our device;
That Falstaff at that oak shall meet with us,
Disguised, like Herne, with huge horns on his head.

(from 'The Merry Wives of Windsor' Act IV Scene IV)

However, the name Horne may be a remnant of the genuine legend. In Jutland there is a legend of Horns Jaeger (Horn the Hunter) who rides at night and hunts female trolls in the woods and fields.

The Well of St. Mary at Pilleth in Lancashire is "reputed to be haunted by a stag-headed former tenant" (Kightly, "The Customs and Ceremonies of Britain", p. 231). Perhaps this apparition represents a local memory of a pagan stag-god, who may have been Herne or a local variant of him. The water of the well is reputed to cure sore eyes and skin complaints.

The tradition of southern England known as the Skimmington Ride may also have been in Shakespeare's mind when he devised Falstaff's punishment. In Devon, the Skimmington Ride took the form of dressing the victim (a man or woman who had been unfaithful to or ill-treated their spouse) as a stag, and pursuing them with mounted huntsmen and lads dressed as dogs.

He may also have been referring obliquely to the myth of Actaeon. In Renaissance thinking, Actaeon's punishment was seen as deserved. (Shakespeare was certainly aware of it because he refers to it in "Twelfth Night", I, i.) The translation by Golding of Ovid's 'Metamorphoses' has Diana sprinkling Actaeon with water from the spring, and the first phase of his transformation was the sprouting of hart's horns on his head. Also, in the sixteenth century, Actaeon was a slang name for a cuckold.

However, the play was written for a Windsor audience, who would certainly have been aware of the local legend of Herne, and it was the pre-existing legend which would have suggested a similarity with Actaeon and given Shakespeare the material for his play.

Herne's Oak at Windsor was felled in 1796, among other trees which were dead. George III had ordered them to be cut down, but he was very upset when he realised that Herne's Oak had been among them. Afterwards the wood from the tree was in great demand, and people made small pieces of furniture and ornaments from it. Subsequently the lie of the land was altered, because the pit nearby was used as a repository for rubbish from the rebuilding of the castle in 1838. In the same year, Edward Jesse suggested that an oak in the avenue was the true oak. When this tree was blown down in a storm, Queen Victoria had another one planted where it had been. In 1906, the avenue was widened, and the tree was removed, but Edward VII planted a new oak on the original site, in the middle of the Home Park. It is, unfortunately, inaccessible to the general public.

It is clear that oaks were sacred in Berkshire from the derivation of the county's name. It comes from the Anglo-Saxon bearu-ac-scire (grove-[of]-oak-shire), from the name of an oak tree near a box grove in Windsor Forest. Box was probably sacred because it was evergreen, a visible sign of the promise of the renewal of life. Near Chieveley there may have been an oak sacred to Woden, though the reference (in the Cartularium Saxonicum) is slightly uncertain. The Berkshire coat of arms depicts an oak and a stag. Michael Drayton's poem of the battle of Agincourt, written in 1627, refers to this:

"Barkshire a Stag, under an Oake that stood
Oxford a White Bull wading in a flood."

Both the Anglo-Saxons and the continental Germanic peoples regarded the stag as a symbol of kingly power and political authority. For example, the royal standard at Sutton Hoo is crowned with a bronze stag. Woden (from whom the Anglo-Saxon kings claimed descent) was led to the halls of the troll-queen Hulda by a deer. In at least two extant texts, Odin himself was referred to as an elk or a stag.

The Herne legend bears a strong similarity to other deer-related myths and customs. Herne is described as walking about the oak "all the winter time". The Kentish Hoodening and the hobby horse dances took place between New Year's Day and Twelfth Night. One of the dancers rode upon the image of a horse (could this be Odin's horse Sleipnir?), making a snapping noise with a bow and arrow in time to the music, while six others danced the hay and other dances with reindeers' heads on their shoulders. They also made as much noise as possible with whips, whistles, chains, and horns. A similar custom appears in Norway, where the dancers are called the Jolesveinar, and in Germany, where they are called Perchten. Similarly to the Hoodeners, Herne is said to shake a chain "in a most hideous and dreadful manner". There is also a link with Odin here, in that a Swabian tribe which worshipped him had a sacred grove which could only be entered by supplicants bound in chains, as a sign of humility and reverence for the god's power.

Other lines of Shakespeare's description also have parallels in Northern Tradition myths: he 'blasts the tree', and the stag Eikthyrni consumes the branches of Yggdrasil; he 'makes the milch kine yield blood', and Frey (god of fertility) was slain with the antlers of a deer. All these customs and legends probably derive ultimately from Mesolithic hunting magic. Drawings of stags have also been found in prehistoric graves, so it appears that they were associated with the dead from the very earliest times.

Despite attempts to link it with the Christian devil, the Wild Hunt continued to be associated with pagan deities. Both Berchta and Holda were said to ride in the wild cavalcade, and Diana and Herodias were said to be associated with it. In ancient Greece and Rome, Hecate and Diana were associated with the hosts of the dead. In India, the antlered god Rudra leads the Maruts, a host of the dead, and is also Lord of the Animals. The Germanic names of the Wild Hunt associate it with Odin, or with raging, which is the origin of his name:

> *Wuedens Jagd* (Hessia)
> *Wodensheer* (Mecklenburg)
> *Woedende Jager* - raging hunt (Netherlands)
> *Odinsjagt* (Denmark)

In Lower Saxony and Brandenburg, the leader of the hunt is called the Nachtfuhrmann (night carter). In North Germany, the wild hunt is called the English Hunt; this probably refers to an ancient belief that the souls of the dead were ferried across the Channel to Britain.

Another leader of the wild hunt was Wild Edric, according to Shropshire legend. He was a Saxon ealdorman who resisted William the Conqueror, because he had been dispossessed of his lands by the Norman Conquest. He was said to be condemned to wander, unable to die, with his followers, because he gave up the resistance too soon. He was supposed to ride out from the Shropshire hills in the direction of enemy territory before the outbreak of war. He was sighted in 1853 or 1854, just before the Crimean War, by a Rorrington miner and his daughter. They heard the sound of a hunting horn. The miner told his daughter to cover her face and to keep quiet until the ghostly cavalcade had gone past, otherwise she would go mad. But she managed to see something of them - Edric was mounted on a white horse and carried a hunting horn in his hand. He had dark curly hair and black eyes, and wore a short green coat and cloak, a green cap with a white feather, and a short sword. Lady Godda, his wife, was also dressed in green, with a dagger at her waist, and a white linen band round her forehead with a gold ornament. Her hair was loose, golden, and wavy. Wild Edric was also supposed to haunt the Shropshire lead mines with his followers (known as the Old Men); the sound of their knocking was the sign of a good lode. Although there have been no recorded appearances of Wild Edric since the Crimean War, the Shropshire lead miners apparently had prior knowledge of wars. Another legend tells that Edric took a fairy wife. He was also associated with a fish in Bomere Pool near Shrewsbury which wore his sword at its side and could not be caught with any net. It was said to have received the sword in trust when Edric disappeared. It was probably the guardian spirit of the pool. The Hunter is often identified with kings or noblemen who were guilty of some crime, and therefore condemned to lead the hunt. This may hark back to the connection of Woden with the cult of kingship.

In Sweden, the wild hunt was seen in the nineteenth century. There the quarry was a white hind and a naked woman with a huge sagging stomach, pursued by hounds and hunters. In another part of Sweden, the quarry is St. Walpurga, who is hunted for nine nights culminating in May Eve. Bonfires are lit on 30th April to protect her from the hunter. Her attributes are a golden crown, a distaff, a wheatsheaf, and a three-cornered mirror which gives glimpses of the future. The last sheaf of the harvest is dedicated to her, and three crosses, a triangle, or a tripod are cut in the bark of trees with an axe to ward off the hunter. She sounds remarkably similar to the goddess Frigga.

The Horselberg in Thuringia (where Tannhauser encountered Venus) is said to be a hill from which the wild hunt sallies forth. Armies of the dead are supposed to sleep in hills, to emerge in time of need to save their country. There are Arthur and his knights, Redbeard and Friedrich Barbarossa in Germany, Holger Dansk in Denmark, Queen Jadwiga in Poland, and Prince Marko in Serbia. On ancient battle sites, ghostly armies clash on the anniversary of the battle; their spirits are said to be unable to rest.

The dead often ride out on Roman roads. (I have seen the ghostly cavalcade myself on an old Roman road.) In Anglo-Saxon charters of Berkshire, "host-paths" were identified in various places, often following the route of an old Roman road. The appearance of the hunt is often heralded by a clap of thunder, the noise of wind in the trees, ghostly music, the ringing of bells, the rattle of chains, the baying of hounds, the clash of swords, the whinnying and stamping of horses, the shouts of the huntsmen, and the sound of the hunting-horn. Its disappearance is preceded by an increase in its noise followed by a complete silence, or a column of fire, the breaking of a storm, the swaying of treetops. It often disappears at cock-crow or sunrise. It is most likely to appear at midnight of Midwinter and during the twelve nights of Christmas, especially if there is stormy weather, but it will also appear at Midsummer and at the Spring and Autumn Equinoxes. Sometimes it is preceded by an old man with a staff in his hand, who is sometimes known as honest Eckart, who blows a horn or utters a warning:

> "Fly then, quickly, make no stay
> For Herne the Hunter rides this way."

On the occasion when I saw the Wild Hunt, around Midsummer 1991, I was walking with two companions on the Roman road near Wandlebury in Cambridgeshire, and remarked that there was a remarkable weight of history on that road. Shortly afterwards we saw a procession of robed and hooded figures, led by a similar figure with a staff. They were on foot and completely silent. When they had passed by, we felt as if the forest went on forever, leading into the forests of the other world, and that we could easily follow them into that other world if we went astray.

There is often a wagon with the hunt, which occasionally needs repair by an earthly wainwright; he is usually paid handsomely for his services. This may be connected with the constellation known as Charles' Wain (Anglo-Saxon carleswaen). Some of the riders of the hunt are deformed, with limbs or an eye missing, or they carry their heads under their arms. Some of them have the head of a stag. Sometimes the hunt is accompanied by the hunger harrow, which is a portent of a bad harvest. It was seen in Sweden in the 1860s, covered in black birds and flying high in the air. In other accounts the hunt is preceded by a worn-out broom or a pair of shoes which lead anyone who puts them on astray. Sometimes the hunt is followed by a lame goose which has difficulty keeping up with it. Dogs of various shapes and sizes are seen with the Hunt, and occasionally stray into other legends. Robin Hood's Well at Wakefield is supposed to be the haunt of a barguest or padfoot known as the Boggart of Longar Hede. It is a spectral hound with saucer eyes, and a chain on one hind leg. It was followed by a sound like a pack of hounds in full cry, and was regarded as a death omen by all who saw it. This apparition would appear to be a remnant of the Wild Hunt. Various other spectral hounds, ghostly coaches, headless riders, etc., may be remnants of the Wild Hunt.

Hunting

According to Dumezil, there are three social functions common to Indo-European cultures:

oratores, men of prayer (cf. brahmin)
bellatores, men of war (cf. kshatriya)
laboratores, men of labour (cf. sudra)

The warrior aristocracy attempted to appropriate the forest for a private hunting ground, but they had to share it with the men of prayer (saints and hermits), and the peasants gathering food, fuel, building materials, and honey, and grazing their livestock there. All these groups went to the forest fleeing from 'culture' (in every sense of the word), reverting to a hunter-gatherer state. However, the hermits were probably not very popular with the hunters, as they sheltered hunted animals in their caves and huts (a kind of early hunt sabotage).

A complex ethos was developed by the hunters; they developed the metaphor of the love-hunt. This could be either God hunting for lost souls, or the knight pursuing his lady-love. Parallels were also drawn with Diana and Actaeon (see section on the Greeks).

The hunters were also possessed of a great deal of forest lore. They knew how to survive in the forest, and how to track animals, and how to cut them up when they had killed them. This was known as the art of venery.

The Forest as Refuge

The medieval forest was a refuge for pagan cults, hermits, those defeated in war, fugitive serfs, murderers, soldiers of fortune, outlaws, exiles, and brigands. Robin Hood and his Merrie Men epitomise the wild and free life of the forest outlaw. They are also subversives, robbing the rich to give to the poor. This reversal of the order of things was a popular element in folk festivities, from the Saturnalia of ancient Rome to the Lord of Misrule in medieval festivals. The fugitive from the harsh justice of the Norman rulers could flee to the vast expanses of forest, and from there, conduct a sporadic guerrilla war against the authorities. The peasants were always willing to help these fugitives or to lend an ear to their tales of the merry life of the greenwood. In 'Yvain, ou le Chevalier au Lion', the forest is both a refuge for the mad, the locus of the hero's madness, and the means by which his personality is reintegrated.

The Forest in Literature

The forest is the location of the action in many medieval epic poems. The romances of Chretien de Troyes (especially 'Yvain', 'Perceval', and 'Aucassin et Nicolette'), Beroul's 'Tristan', the *chansons de geste*, and the work of the Occitan troubadour Bernard Marti were some of the French poems dealing with the theme of exile and adventure in the forest. This theme appeared in English poetry in 'Sir Gawain and the Green Knight' and 'Sir Orfeo', which were both written by the same poet in an alliterative style.

In the *chansons de geste*, the forest was originally depicted as a place in which noble warriors could hunt. In 'Le Moniage Guillaume' (a *chanson de geste* of the latter half of the twelfth century), which deals with the last years in the life of the hero Guillaume d'Orange when he becomes a monk and then a hermit, the forest becomes a place of hermits "in the depths of the leafy wood". The nobleman takes refuge there because he is sick of killing people in a country ravaged by war; the warrior becomes a man of prayer. Many late twelfth century works depicted the forest as a place to flee from the world of the warrior aristocracy, whose ascendancy had begun to be threatened by the beginnings of a new society. Examples of these are 'Renaud de Montauban (Les Quatre Fils Aymon)' and 'Girard de Roussillon'.

Medieval European literature drew on two sources: the Judaeo-Christian tradition; and the Northern Tradition of the Pagan Celts, Germans, Franks, etc. One such source was Snorri Sturluson's Icelandic saga of Harald Sigurdson. At the beginning of the saga the exiled Harald hides in the house of a peasant in the forest. The peasant's son guides him through the forest. In this saga the forest is seen as a trial which must be undergone; but there is also the familiar theme of the exiled king, and the person familiar with the forest who guides him. The Judaeo-Christian tradition, on the other hand, had been accustomed to see the wilderness as a refuge. These two traditions merged to form a complex image of the forest as both a place to hide and a place of danger.

In courtly literature, the forest was the setting for the chivalric adventure story. In Béroul's 'Tristan', Tristan and Isolde flee the wrath of King Mark and take refuge in the forest of Morois. Here Tristan "feels as safe as in a castle surrounded by walls". He is an excellent archer, so is able to hunt for food for himself and Isolde; and he builds a cabin for their dwelling. Here they remain "deep in the forest, a desert in which they remained for a long time". Here the various themes come into play: the forest as refuge, the forest as desert or wilderness, and the forest associated with the bow and arrow (which is connected with the archetype of the divine huntsman, a common Indo-European image). The couple are not discovered in the forest for a long time, because of people's fear of the forest. They meet a hermit, however, who causes them to repent of their sins. Tristan perfects a bow which never misses its target, and they live on wild game. They eat no bread (this generally symbolised being uncivilised, as bread is a product of agriculture). Eventually the forest warden (who protects the king's rights in the forest) denounces them to King Mark. The king forswears vengeance, but since they have been discovered, Tristan and Isolde leave the forest, which is no longer a refuge for them.

In Chrétien de Troyes' poem 'Yvain', the hero goes mad after being spurned by his wife because he fails to keep a promise to her. The story opens with an account of another knight attempting to defeat Esclados le Roux, the guardian of a magic fountain at the heart of the forest of Broceliande. After Yvain's wife has rejected him, he flees the court of King Arthur and takes refuge in the forest. His flight is a symbolic descent into madness: as the landscape becomes wilder, so does he. He flees the camp of the knights of the court, passes through fields and hedgerows, into wooded parkland, then into the forest proper.

Whilst in the park (a grazing area at the edge of the forest), he appropriates a bow and some arrows from a servant boy. Once in the forest, he regresses to a state of nature, hunting with the bow and arrows, and eating raw meat. The bow and arrow was not considered a knightly weapon, since it allowed the combatant to avoid direct contact with his opponent; its use in war was considered unchivalrous, though its use in hunting was heroic. It was either the weapon of the solitary hunter, or a royal symbol, the attribute of a super-hero (such as Arjuna, Ulysses, or Roland). Yvain meets two people during his sojourn in the wilderness, a wild man and a hermit. The wild man, a "hideous base fellow covered in hair", wears animal skins and has control over two bulls; he appears to be derived from the Celtic Lord of the Animals. The hermit lives in a hut, clears land by burning, buys and eats bread, and cooks his food.

There is a clear hierarchy of wildness presented here: the hairy man is completely at one with nature; Yvain is temporarily outcast from society; and the hermit is wild but partially civilised, and he aspires to higher things. A psychoanalyst would say that the wild man represents the id, or instinctive drives; the hero is the ego struggling for integration; and the hermit is the superego, that which yearns for the spiritual. The wild man and the hermit are also presented as alternative solutions for Yvain: he can become completely wild like the hairy man, or he can learn from the hermit, who will help him to be rehabilitated into civilisation. (Many ordinary people went to hermits for confession, healing, advice, and blessing. Kings often consulted them, as the forest was a royal domain. However, they would also give advice to outlaws. One such relationship is that of Friar Tuck and Robin Hood; another such is depicted in the English fable 'The Eremyte and the Outlawe'.) To return to the story of Yvain, however, he wins through various ordeals, eventually regains his sanity, and is reunited with his wife. One of his ordeals is to fight Esclados le Roux, the guardian of the magic fountain at the heart of the forest (a similar motif to the King of Nemi in Frazer's 'The Golden Bough'). He defeats and slays Esclados and marries his widow, with the magical assistance of her maid Lunette.

In 'The Story of the Grail (the Romance of Perceval)' by Chretien de Troyes, the forest is depicted as a place of trial and adventure. It is also described as a place of great beauty, which is unusual in the poetry of the twelfth century.

"... It was in the season when the trees break into leaf, when iris plants and woods and meadows become green, when the birds in their own language sing sweetly in the morning, when everything is aflame with joy, that the son of the widow of the wild and lonely forest arose; it was no trouble to him to saddle his horse and take three darts; and thus he went out from his mother's dwelling. ... And so he went out into the forest; and immediately his heart was glad within him for the lovely weather and the song he heard from the rejoicing birds; all these things pleased him."

Perceval is the son of the Lady of the Forest Waste; he is not a savage in the true sense of the word, he is an innocent, like the Fool of the Tarot card. When he hears some knights coming towards him through the forest, making a great noise, "for often the branches of the oaks and the hornbeams clashed against their armour, and the lances struck against the shields, and all the hauberks jingled", he thinks at first that they are devils, but when he sees how splendid they are, thinks that they must be God and some of his angels. His initiatory journey through the forest includes meditation, adventure, and lonely wandering. Sometimes the forest is called lonely, false, and treacherous, a place of hallucinations, temptations, and ambushes. At the crucial moment Perceval encounters a hermit, who explains the meaning of all the trials he has undergone.

The theme of the forest as a place of trial and refuge is also found in Chretien de Troyes' poem 'Aucassin et Nicolette'. Nicolette flees into an immense and frightening forest, fearful of being eaten alive by its wild denizens. Once there she overcomes her fear and builds a hut. Aucassin follows her, and encounters a wild-looking peasant who is in the forest searching for his ox. Eventually the lovers traverse the forest, come to the sea, and return to civilisation.

The troubadours turned the theme of the lovers' flight into the forest into an idyllic voluntary retreat into a sylvan utopia, a desert of love.

> " ... I want to live as a hermit in the woods, provided my lady comes with me. There we shall sleep beneath a coverlet of leaves. This is where I wish to live and die. I abandon and renounce all other cares."
>
> (Bernard Marti)

In all these tales, the forest is presented as the antithesis of the city. The forest is associated with solitude, refuge, initiation, trials, a retreat into the wilderness. The city is associated with civilisation, the castle, King Arthur's court, crowds of people. The hero goes into the forest on a journey of self-discovery, and returns to the city with the inner resources to be able to participate fully in the life of civilisation. Kings went to the forests for renewal, to hunt or to consult hermits; reforging their link with the source of holiness and legitimacy, which was the wild land of the forest. This journey of self-discovery reached its apogee in the Grail legends, where the knights went on strange and perilous journeys in search of the Grail. Only those who were worthy could continue the quest, and their adventures were the test of their worth. Ultimately the Grail came to be identified with the Philosopher's Stone. The journey of the Grail knight could be identified with the Great Work of the alchemists. Both were an initiatory journey into the depths of the psyche to find the true self.

In antiquity, the contrast had been between the city and the country (urbs and rus); in the Middle Ages, the contrast was between nature and culture. Nature was seen as that which was essentially wild (desert, forest, ocean, and wilderness), and culture was seen as that which was built, cultivated, and inhabited (cities, castles, villages, and fields).

In English literature, the forest theme was taken up by the unknown fourteenth-century author of "Sir Gawain and the Green Knight" and "Sir Orfeo". He used the forest as a wilderness setting for the initiatory experiences of his heroes, but included the wilder elements of myth, strange encounters with the world of faerie.

In "Sir Gawain and the Green Knight", the court of King Arthur is about to commence the Christmas feast when a knight clad all in green, with a green face and a green beard, rides into the hall and requests that one of the knights deal him a blow with his axe, provided that he may deal another stroke in return, which he will delay for a year and a day. King Arthur is prepared to take up the challenge, but Gawain asks him to let him do it. So he hews off the Green Knight's head, and all present are horrified to see the knight pick up his head, which he holds under his arm. The Green Knight then reminds Gawain of his promise to seek him out in a year and a day to be dealt the return stroke. A year passes and Gawain sets out to find the Green Chapel; he rides through great forests and tracts of wilderness, till he finally comes to a castle, where he is welcomed by the knight who dwells there. He is told that the Green Chapel is only a short distance away, and is invited to spend Christmas in the castle. The lord proposes that Gawain stay there while he is out hunting, and that they exchange whatever trophies they win at the end of each day. Each day the lady of the castle tries to seduce Gawain, but he resists her advances, and at the end of each day he gives the lord of the castle the kisses she has given him in exchange for the spoils of the chase. On the third day, however, the lady gives him a magic girdle which will protect the wearer from all wounds; this gift he does not give to the knight, but keeps for himself.

Finally he rides out to keep his tryst with the Green Knight, who gives him a blow with the axe, but only makes a small cut in his neck. He then reveals himself to be one and the same as the knight in whose castle Gawain has been staying, and to have set his wife to seduce Gawain to test his loyalty. He himself was transformed into the Green Knight by Morgan le Fay, who wished to test the valour of the knights of King Arthur. Gawain is ashamed that he kept the girdle, and vows to wear it always to remind him of his disloyalty. When he returns to the court, he tells the whole story, and the rest of the court decide to wear a green girdle also, for love of Gawain.

Some have seen in this story a reworking of an ancient myth associated with the winter solstice, a ritual combat between two gods of fertility. The Green Knight, clad all in green, with a holly-bundle in one hand and his axe in the other, can be identified with the Holly King (the King of the Waning Year), who must be killed in order for the Waxing Year to triumph. The original form of Gawain's name appears to be Gwalchmai, the Hawk of May. He represents the waxing year.

In "Sir Orfeo", the hero is a king whose wife, Heurodis, is strolling in the orchard one day when she and her maidens fall asleep beneath a grafted tree. There she dreams that a faery host comes to her and demands that she accompany them to the Otherworld, else they will rend her limb from limb. She is greatly grieved, and tears her hair. The next day Orfeo and a hundred knights accompany her to the tree, but she is snatched from their midst all unawares. Then Orfeo in his grief renounces his throne, sets a steward to reign in his stead, and becomes a wandering harper. He roams the forests eating roots and berries, still grieving for Heurodis. Sometimes he sees the faery host ride by, and one day he sees sixty faery women, among whom Heurodis rides. She recognises him and sheds tears for his lowly state, but they dare not speak, and the ladies make her ride away. But Orfeo follows them, and when they ride into a rock, he follows them, until they come to the castle of the faery king. He seeks admission as a wandering minstrel, and his harping is so beautiful that the king offers him anything he wants. He asks for Heurodis, and taking her by the hand, leaves the faery realms. They return to their own kingdom, and Orfeo goes to his steward still dressed as a beggar. When he plays his harp the steward recognises it and asks him how he got it. Orfeo tells him that he found it by the body of a man killed by lions, whereupon the steward grieves deeply for the death of his king. Having thus tested the steward's loyalty, Orfeo reveals himself, is restored to his throne, and promises the kingdom to the steward after his death.

The interesting thing about this story is that it is a reworking of Orpheus' journey to the underworld in search of Eurydice in an English setting. It has a happy ending instead of a tragic one, the realm of faery instead of the underworld, and abduction by the faeries instead of death. In another context, Nigel Aldcroft Jackson has suggested that the faeries and the spirits of the dead are one and the same. That being so, the transposition of the events of the story would have seemed perfectly reasonable to a fourteenth century audience. The poem includes descriptions of the forest as a desolate waste, the locus of madness and despair. There is also an interesting description of the unfortunate mortals abducted by the faeries, among whom Heurodis sleeps beneath the grafted tree.

Another medieval English romance which includes the themes of the exiled prince and the faithful lovers reunited after a long separation is the story of King Horn. Horn is exiled from his kingdom by an invasion, and falls in love with the princess Rymenild, from whom he is separated by the treachery of a rival. After many trials and setbacks, the lovers are reunited and Horn's kingdom is restored to him. The story is related to the romance of Horn Childe and Maiden Rimnild (Auchinleck MS, 14th century), and the Scottish ballads of Hind Horn. It is generally believed to have originated around the time of the Danish invasions. It includes descriptions of hunting, and much of the action takes place in the forest.

Medieval Forestry

The forest was seen as a resource. It was a game preserve; a source of food, fuel, honey (used for making mead and sweetening food), wax for candles, and building timber; it could be used for grazing animals (e.g. pigs eating acorns and beech mast); and it was a source of materials for making glass and refining metal. In the Forest of Dean there were mines. However, the forest was also seen as wild and dangerous, and the people who lived there were seen as frightening and wild by ordinary people. There were hunters, charcoal burners, blacksmiths, honey and wax gatherers, ashmen producing glass and soap, bark pullers (bark was used in tanning leather and making rope), as well as the hermits, wild men, and outlaws.

The inhospitable nature of the forest was legendary; in Emperor Henry IV's war with the Saxons, he had great difficulty in finding his way out of the huge and terrible German forest; he and his companions nearly died of hunger. Unless one was a hunter with knowledge of the secrets of the forest, it was a very frightening place.

Forest Law

In Britain, the forest was a place where feudal law broke down. In theory, it was replaced by forest law. The law of the forest came "not from the common law of the kingdom but from the will of the prince, so that it was said that what was done according to these laws was not just in an absolute sense but according to the law of the forest." (*De necessariis observantiis scaccarii dialogus.*) Similarly, in Provence, judicial language made a distinction between privati (people dwelling within the ramparts) and *extranei* or *forestieri* (people residing in hamlets outside the city and forest inhabitants not integrated into the community).

William the Conqueror laid claim to large tracts of forest as royal hunting preserves (the Saxon Kings had had hunting rights beyond the royal demesne, but they were not exclusive). Forest law was established in these areas, ensuring the protection of game and trees from all but the King, who had sole hunting, felling, and mineral rights. However, he could and did lease them to others. Denizens of the forest could only fell wood for their personal use, and were not allowed to assart the land (convert it to agricultural use). Forest law was first defined by a statute of 1184 known as the Assize of Woodstock.

The medieval definition of the forest was a large area preserved by royal decree as hunting grounds for the king. Such areas could include whole towns and villages. Examples of medieval 'forests' which would not be regarded as such today are the Forest of Bowland in Lancashire, Exmoor, and Dartmoor.

The modern definition of a forest is a large tract of land, mostly trees, which may include heathland (such as the New Forest in Hampshire). A wood is defined as a mixed species tract of trees, not planted, which includes underbrush. A plantation is a planted tract of trees, usually of a single species.

The royal forests were administered by a group of officials responsible to the king. Before 1229, there was one post of the King's chief forester. After 1229, there were two: one responsible for the forests north of the River Trent, one for the forests south of it. In 1222, there were 34 royal forests. The most important of these were the Forest of Dean, the New Forest, Rockingham Forest, Savernake, Pickering, Witchwood, and Selwood.

Individual royal forests were governed by a keeper, steward, warden, or master forester (occasionally a hereditary post). The warden's deputy was the lieutenant of the forest. The lieutenant had charge of up to six verderers, usually a position for life held by a knight elected by local freeholders. Verderers kept records of the people accused of breaches of forest law, and brought them to a special court called a swainmote for the preliminary hearing. The judgment was delivered by a higher court called the eyre. The verderers also had charge of numerous foresters, who were responsible for the vert (trees) and venison (deer and wild boar) and for arresting people found hunting in the forest.

There were also foresters-of-fee (a hereditary post), mostly gentleman guardians of the forest. The area administered by a forester was called a bailiwick or a walk. Foresters on horseback had larger bailiwicks, as they could cover a greater area. Woodwards were employed by private owners of woodland, but they also had to ensure that the king's rights were respected. There were also forest agisters who regulated herbage (grazing) and pannage (pigs eating acorns etc.) and collected rents for this. In the mid-fourteenth century, the first record of rangers appears; they looked after purlieus (the disafforested areas within the forest) and drove deer back into the forested areas from the open land. Enclosed forest deer parks were managed by parkers, who may also have had charge of palers, who constructed and repaired the park's pale, or fence. There were also regarders, who surveyed all aspects of forest management (grazing, woods, buildings, boundaries, and the conduct of forest officials) and presented their report (called a regard) to the eyre every year. The eyre consisted of at least twelve men of standing, usually knights. However, eyres met very irregularly, so much so that an accused person had often died before their case came to court. At the height of forest law, however, the punishments meted out were severe, and it was in this atmosphere that the legend of Robin Hood flourished.

Sacred Trees

In Pagan times, the felling of a sacred tree was an offence punishable by death. The evidence for this is in the song "The Two Brothers", in which a man kills his brother for pulling up a sacred tree:

> "And what did you two fall out about,
> My son come tell to me?
> Oh it was that he plucked up a little hazel bush
> That should have grown to a tree tree tree
> That should have grown to a tree."

There is a story that Bishop Otto of Bamberg (the Apostle of Pomerania) ordered a spruce tree in Stettin to be cut down, because the Pagans believed their gods dwelt in it, and the people made obeisance to it as they passed. The people begged the bishop not to have the tree felled, promising on oath never to do pagan homage to it again, because they liked the tree for its beauty and the shade which it gave.

The Glastonbury Thorn (Crataegus monogyna 'Praecox') has long been regarded as a sacred tree; any damage to it would result in harm to the perpetrator. A Puritan who tried to cut it down in the seventeenth century was blinded in one eye by a flying wood-chip. The tree was said to have grown from Joseph of Arimathea's staff, which he stuck in the ground in token that he would end his wanderings there. It blossomed on Christmas Day, and continues to do so. Another tradition has it that it sprang from one of the thorns in the Crown of Thorns, also brought by St. Joseph.

There are several other thorn trees in Europe which are said to have sprung from the Crown of Thorns, which flower miraculously on Good Friday. The Holy Thorn at Andria in Italy is said to change colour every seventy years, when Good Friday and the Feast of the Annunciation fall on the same day. The last occurrence of this was on 26th March 1932. The tree, usually dry and greyish, turned green and moist, and had dark blood-coloured stains on it. (This story is strongly reminiscent of certain attributes of Osiris.)

When the English calendar was changed from the Julian to the Gregorian system in 1752, two thousand people went to Quainton in Buckinghamshire, where there was a tree which was supposed to have grown from a slip of the Holy Thorn at Glastonbury, to see if it would flower on the new Christmas Day. When it did not do so, they continued to celebrate the festival according to the old calendar. A similar crowd assembled at Glastonbury, where the thorn flowered on Old Christmas Day (5th January according to the Gregorian calendar).

Various other trees were also supposed to have grown miraculously from a staff planted in the ground. All these stories closely resemble legends of a vegetation cult which continued into Christian times, with the miraculous occurrences being attributed to saints instead of being ascribed to Pagan deities. Odin was said to have a 'ragged staff', an ash stave which continually budded and bloomed; these legends are a continuation of the same theme.

St. Aldhelm thrust his ash stave into the ground, and it miraculously budded, so he left it there. The town in Wiltshire where this happened is now called Bishopstrow (from Anglo-Saxon treow, a tree). Many ash trees sprang from the original tree.

At Stow in Lincolnshire, St. Etheldreda and her maidens, being weary, lay down to rest. St. Etheldreda stuck her staff in the ground. When they awoke, the staff had rooted and put forth leaves and branches to shield the saint from the sun.

At Guimaraes in Portugal, the people met to elect a king, and their choice fell on a man called Wamba. He resolved not to accept, and stuck his ironshod staff of olive wood into the ground, swearing by the Four Evangelists never to reign until it should blossom, which it promptly did. Thinking this was witchcraft, he tried to pull it from the ground, but it had taken root, so he fell to his knees and prayed for wisdom and valour to govern the country well. Similarly, St. Cannat of Marseilles refused to become bishop, swearing only to do so if the staff he stuck in the ground should blossom. It also blossomed, so he became bishop. His feast-day is celebrated by decorating the church with staves adorned with flowers.

The staff of St. Polycarp grew into a cherry tree, which is a venerated relic at Smyrna; the staff of St. Francis, which grew into an oak tree, is still venerated near Venice. After St. Christopher carried Christ across the river, he was commanded to plant his staff in the ground. Next morning it was a palm tree with leaves and fruit. St. Brigid's staff flowered when she was professed as a nun; the staff of Papas the Martyr blossomed when he was killed. St. Athanasius of Athos was commanded by the Virgin to strike a rock with his staff; a stream gushed out from the spot, and he thrust his staff into the ground, where it produced boughs and leaves.

A similar tale is related in the Bible (Numbers 17). Aaron's staff "had not only sprouted but had budded, blossomed, and produced almonds." This was a sign that Yahweh had chosen him and his tribe to offer incense; no-one else was allowed to do so.

Islamic legend tells that Mohammed planted his staff at Medina; it grew into a palm tree.

Another miraculous staff appears in the legend of Tannhauser, who was a minnesinger at the court of Frederick II, Duke of Austria, and Otto II, Duke of Bavaria, and went on the Fifth Crusade (1228). Legend has it that Tannhauser accidentally found his way into the cavern of Horselberg, the dwelling of the goddess Venus. He spent seven delightful years with her, which passed as if they were one night. Then he heard the sound of church bells far away, and repented, but Venus would not let him go, so he called on the Virgin Mary for help. He immediately found himself on the upper earth again, and went to the Pope to seek absolution. The Pope was horrified by the tale and said "Sooner shall this dry staff of mine bud and blossom again, than that God should forgive thee!" So Tannhauser went away despairing, and was last seen heading towards the Venusberg. Three days later, the Pope's staff budded, so he sent messengers after Tannhäuser into every land, but they could not find him, and he was never seen again.

In Virgil's 'Aeneid' (XII, 206-211), Latinus swears an oath on his staff, on the grounds that breaking his word is about as likely as his staff putting forth branches. A similar oath is sworn by Achilles in Homer's 'Iliad' (I, 233-237).

The Frankish Christian army of Charlemagne was fighting the Saracens in Spain. The night before the battle they planted their spears in the ground, and the next morning they were covered in bark and branches. They cut them off close to the ground, and the roots that were left there sprouted afresh and became lofty trees.

An immense tree once stood at Nannau in North Wales. It was called the Spirit's Blasted Tree. It was destroyed by lightning in 1813. Legend has it that the Abbot of Cwmmer tried to reconcile Owain Glyndwr and Howel Sele, who were sworn enemies, despite being kinsfolk. But Owain shot Howel with an arrow and hid the body in this hollow tree. In spite of a thorough search, it was not found until forty years later. The place was dreaded by country folk as an abode of evil spirits.

There is an oak at Carmarthen called Merlin's Oak; according to legend, when the tree falls, so will the town.

The oak tree which was struck by Tyrrel's arrow when he killed William Rufus was said to put forth leaves at midwinter. Another oak tree at Cadenham (a few miles from Lyndhurst in the New Forest), which was a forest boundary tree, became green on Old Christmas Day (5th January in the Gregorian calendar) but was leafless before and after. This may be derived from the association of Yule with turning points, both spatial and temporal; as the solstice is the shortest day, after which the light returns, it was natural to associate it with boundaries, which are places where one turns back.

Marriage oaks, though forbidden by the Church, survived a long time. There was one at Brampton in Cumberland until the mid-nineteenth century. Newlyweds hurried from the church porch, danced three times round the oak, and cut a cross in the bark. This is probably a survival of a Pagan marriage custom.

THE RENAISSANCE

Renaissance art and thought used Pagan mysteries allegorically and symbolically. Pagan deities were understood as expressing inner truth (e.g. the psychopomp). However, the concern of Renaissance writers was less with the original meaning of the Pagan mystery cults than with adapting them to the philosophy of their own age.

For example, the flaying of Marsyas was seen as a conflict between Apollonian clarity and Dionysian darkness. Marsyas' flute was a Dionysiac instrument which roused the dark passions of the unconscious; by contrast, the lyre of Apollo was seen as an instrument of purity, appealing to the intellect. The flaying was seen as a tragic ordeal of purification, since the satyr represented instinct, and the purification revealed the beauty of the inner self. The agonised cry of Marsyas, 'Why do you tear me from myself?' ('*Quid me mihi detrahis?*') expresses the experience of initiation.

A frequently used symbol of the Renaissance itself was the renascent tree, depicted as a fresh shoot growing from a dry tree. This was also used to symbolise religious rebirth.

Trees in Alchemy

Paracelsus linked Woman, the Earth, and the Tree together as the Mysterium Magnum, thus harking back to ancient concepts of the Great Mother being embodied by the Tree of Life:

"... the Mysterium Magnum which is the one mother of all things and of all elements and a grandmother of all stars, trees, and creatures of the flesh... earth is the "mother" of man who shares "mother earth" with the plants, minerals, and certain spiritual emanations."

"Woman is like the earth and all the elements, and in this sense she must be considered a matrix; she is the tree which grows from the earth, and the child is like the fruit that is born of the tree. Just as a tree stands in the earth and belongs not only to the earth but also to the air and the water and the fire, so all the four elements are in woman - for the Great Field, the lower and the upper sphere of the world consist of these - and in the middle of it stands the tree; woman is the image of the tree."

Trees in the Tarot

The 22 cards of the Major Arcana of the Tarot correspond to the 22 Hebrew letters and the 22 paths of the Kabbalistic Tree of Life.

The aspen tree is said to be associated with the Fool card. The aspen is symbolic of fear, uncertainty, and lamentation, so it could symbolise the Fool's ambivalence about leaping into the unknown.

The Hanged Man card is derived from the shamanic practice of hanging in trees to retrieve esoteric knowledge from the depths (see section on Germanic mysteries of the forest).

Chapter 4

The Festivals

In order to attune ourselves to Nature, we celebrate the cycle of seasonal festivals. There are two cycles within the pattern, the solar cycle and the vegetation cycle. The lunar cycles are celebrated as the 13 full moons in the year. The Great Sabbats (Samhain, Imbolc, Beltane, and Lammas) are sometimes referred to as the lunar festivals, since in some traditions, they were celebrated at the nearest full moon (Hunter's Moon, Spring Moon, May Moon, and Harvest Moon). The solar festivals are the solstices and equinoxes.

The Vegetation Cycle

This can refer to all plants, but here the focus is on trees.

Festival	Stage in cycle
Autumn Equinox	Ripening of fruit; harvest of fruit.
Samhain	Leaves turn gold and fall from tree; seed falls from parent plant.
Yule	Turning point; cold conditions enable seed to germinate. Mature trees dormant; forestry work may be undertaken.
Imbolc	First red twigs indicate start of new growth. Cherry and blackthorn begin to bloom.
Spring Equinox	Seed sprouts; sap rises in mature trees.
Beltane	Leaves fully out; in a good year, hawthorn in blossom.

Midsummer	Flowers are fertilised; beginnings of fruit production.
Lammas	Completion; seeds begin to form.

The eight seasonal festivals can also be associated with specific trees, appropriate to the qualities of the festivals. Others may prefer a different scheme, but my personal attributions for each festival are as follows:

Samhain:	Elder (for the Crone); Apple (fruit of the Underworld)
Yule:	Holly (sacred to Saturn etc.); Mistletoe
Imbolc:	Blackthorn (flowers around Imbolc)
Spring Equinox:	Great Sallow or Goat Willow (Salix caprea), sacred to Freyja.
Beltane:	Hawthorn (flowers around May 1st)
Midsummer:	Oak (sacred to Jupiter etc.)
Lammas:	Gorse (sacred to Lugh); Ivy (often twined round the last sheaf of the harvest).
Autumn Equinox:	Apple (for the cider harvest)

Samhain: 31st October

The festival of Samhain is closely associated with Bonfire Night; the custom of having a bonfire at this time of year antedates the custom of burning an effigy of Guy Fawkes by several centuries. The word bonfire is derived from "bone-fire", since the material used in the fire was originally bone, perhaps the bones of the cattle which had been slaughtered to reduce the size of the herd so that there was enough fodder to go round amongst the remaining cattle, and to provide meat for the tribe or village.

The feast of Samhain was regarded as a time when the boundaries between the worlds of gods and men were thinner than usual; it was a time when people could commune with the dead, drawing on the wisdom of the ancestors, and ascertaining their fate for the coming year. It was the Celtic New Year, the beginning of winter, when the High Kings of Ireland held a week-long feast, and consulted Druids and soothsayers.

In Scotland, Samhain was believed to be a time when the faery folk would migrate from one mound to another, taking the mortals they had captured along with them. Thus Samhain was a time when these mortals could be taken back by their loved ones, as in the ballad "The Young Tamlane" by Sir Walter Scott.

To modern Pagans, it is a time to explore the mysteries of winter; to commune with the ancestors, and to descend into the depths of the psyche, returning with the wisdom of dreams and visions. It is also the time when the Lord of Death and Resurrection emerges from the Forest, and the Goddess takes on the form of the Crone.

In terms of the cycle of vegetation festivals, it is the time when the leaves begin to fall from the trees, and the seed which matured at the Autumnal Equinox falls from the parent plant. The seed then rests in the earth throughout the winter to come.

A Samhain ritual generally encompasses these themes: the Celtic New Year, the slaying of cattle, the falling of the seed from the plant, communing with the spirits of the dead and the winter aspects of the Goddess and the God.

Samhain customs

Apple-bobbing: There are two sorts of apple-bobbing. One is filling a tub with water on which apples are floating, and trying to pick them up with your teeth. This is very difficult and generally involves getting very wet. The apple is traditionally the fruit of the underworld, and the game symbolises the return across the great river of death to the source of all life. It is also great fun!

The other form of the game is to suspend apples on strings, and to try and grab them with your teeth - I don't know what it symbolises, but at least you don't have to get wet!

Mischief Night: All over Britain, children would go out and play pranks on their neighbours (mostly harmless ones such as knocking on doors and running away) on Mischief Night. In Cornwall, it was called Nickanan, and in Devon, it was called Dappy-Door Night; these occurred on Shrove Monday. Over most of the rest of the British Isles, Mischief Night was Hallowe'en or May Eve, when tricks such as blowing smoke through keyholes, blocking chimneys, or whitewashing over windows, could be blamed on mischievous spirits. In Northern England, Mischief Night has been transferred to the evening before Guy Fawkes' Day. This, and the Scottish tradition of Guising, is the origin of the American custom of trick or treat.

Guising: In Scotland Hallowe'en was called Guising, because people would dress in the guise of monsters and legendary characters, and call at every house in the village. This, and the English custom of Mischief Night, is the origin of the American custom of trick or treat. The origin of dressing up was probably the magical custom of dressing as the spirit whose nature the magician needed to understand in order to further personal growth or the welfare of the group. Instead of wearing a mask, some guisers would blacken their faces. An alternative explanation for the custom was that the guiser could go between the worlds without being recognised by the spirits of the dead, and thus could not be trapped in their realms.

Honouring the ancestors: In many countries it is still the custom to visit the graves of loved ones at this time, in the belief that the veil between the worlds is thinner.

Story-telling: This is a traditional pastime of the winter months, because the long period of inaction is a time for reflection, gathering strength for the summer to come. Story-telling helps us to put our lives into perspective, by comparing them with the continually recurring themes of old stories.

A particularly relevant story at Hallowe'en is the legend of Demeter and Persephone, which tells of Persephone's seduction by the lord of the underworld, and her mother Demeter's sorrow at losing her, which causes her to neglect the earth so that winter comes. Eventually a compromise is reached whereby Persephone will spend half the year with her mother and half with her husband, so that it is summer when she is with her mother, but winter when she is in the underworld.

Another relevant story is that of Snow White, whose wicked stepmother is probably derived from the Queen of the Underworld. In some versions of the story, all of the apple which the queen gives to Snow White is poisoned except the core, which the queen eats. This identifies her as Queen of the Underworld, bringing death or radical transformation to those who eat the apple. Subsequently, Snow White's lifeless body is guarded by the Seven Dwarfs (earth or underworld spirits) until she is awoken by the handsome prince (which equates with the festival of Imbolc, when the Goddess returns to the Earth).

Divination and scrying: As the veil between the worlds is thinner at the turn of the year (the old Celtic New Year), this is a good time for divination and scrying. A simple method of scrying is to fill a bowl with water coloured with black ink, and use it as you would a crystal ball. Of course, the simplest way is also the most difficult, and scrying requires an awful lot of perseverance. Runes and Tarot take longer to learn but will produce some information at the first attempt. There were many traditional scrying customs at Hallowe'en, mostly with the aim of discovering the querent's future spouse.

If you are performing a runic divination, it is a good idea to use the following visualisation (idea by D. Jason Cooper, words by the author) before you start.

You are standing on the edge of a great cliff. In front of you is the void between the worlds, a bottomless abyss. From the edge of the cliff, a flaming bridge stretches away into space. It is Bifrost, the Rainbow Bridge. All the colours of the spectrum flicker and burn in its magnificent arc. You walk forward onto the bridge, which, though it is light as gossamer, supports your weight. Beneath you the Nine Worlds are spread out, joined by the tree Yggdrasil. The Rainbow Bridge leads to Asgard, where the three Norns stand by the Well of Wyrd, wherein all time and space is mirrored. One of the Norns, Urd, is a beautiful maiden; she represents the past. The second Norn is Skuld, a gracious lady; she represents the present. The third Norn is Verthandi, a veiled and mysterious crone; she represents the future. Ask them for knowledge of that which has been, that which is, and that which will be. When you have drawn the runes and interpreted them, thank the Norns and return across the Rainbow Bridge.

Isia (Egyptian): 31st October - 3rd November

This was the time when the Seeking and Finding of the body of Osiris was publicly enacted. A black linen vestment was draped over the gilded image of a cow, to signify the mourning Isis. Then the coffin of Osiris was sought high and low. (It occurs to me that the children's game of Hide-and-Seek might have originated with some ancient rite such as this.)

St. Catherine of Sinai (Roman / Egyptian): 25th November

The goddess of the wheel of fate, the turning wheel of the seasons became St. Catherine in Christian iconography. She is depicted holding a burning wheel with eight spokes, similar to the ones rolled downhill at the midsummer bonfire (q.v.)

Festival of Faunus (Roman): 5th December: Nones of December

The cult of Faunus was essentially a rustic element of archaic Roman religion. An attempt was made in 196 BCE to introduce the cult into urban life by establishing a temple in Rome, but it failed. The urban festival was held on 13th February. The rural festival, however, was a lively affair, described in the 'Odes' of Horace. It consisted of dancing in the fields, making an offering of wine and a goat kid to the god on a smoking altar of earth. It expressed the true ancient spirit of Roman religion: "an appeal to the vague and possibly dangerous spirit that guards the flocks to be present, but not to linger too long".

Faunus was essentially the spirit of the wild woodland. (The name is probably derived from 'favere' and means 'the kindly one'.) His father was Picus (the woodpecker), one of the sons of Saturn, and his mother was Canente, who died of grief when Picus was transformed into a woodpecker. Faunus was also the father or husband of Fauna, goddess of Earth and fields, also invoked under the name Bona Dea (the Good Goddess). He protected woods, fields, and shepherds, and was worshipped in sacred groves, where he gave oracles, mostly during sleep, or by causing voices to be heard in the countryside. He was also said to have been a lawgiver and one of the first kings of Latium. His attribute is the shawm or rustic pipe, which he is said to have invented. His sacred tree was the bay laurel (Laurus nobilis), which was also sacred to Silvanus, Mars, Apollo, Ceres, Eros, and Aesculapius.

Yule (21st December)

Yule is derived from the Anglo-Saxon word Geola; the word means "turning point". Yule is the time of the shortest day, when the sun's powers are at their weakest. However, it is also a time of rebirth, because after the shortest day (winter solstice) the days get longer and the sun's power increases. Hence the tradition of the Yule log, which was burnt as a reminder of the sun's fire in the dark days of winter.

In terms of the vegetation cycle the winter solstice is the time when the seed which has fallen from the parent plant begins to germinate. Psychologically, it is the time of enlightenment, the rebirth of the soul after the descent into the underworld.

The Romans celebrated the festival of Saturnalia at this time. At Saturnalia, all normal social conventions were turned upside down: masters served slaves, cross-dressing was rife, and general licentiousness was permissible. Similar customs occurred in medieval times, with the election of boy bishops at Christmas, and the appointment of Lords of Misrule to preside over the general anarchy and merry-making. Saturn was originally a kind of trickster figure, a personification of anarchy; it is only his astrological connotations that make him seem the archetype of misery and suffering. However, there is a connection: the anarchic behaviour permitted at Yule was intended as a temporary respite from the crushing yoke of feudalism and slavery, a way of venting the general frustration with the system - which arguably served to perpetuate the system. Still, we can harness this tradition of anarchic humour today to undermine the status quo, and to free our minds from the strictures imposed by materialism. There is nothing so liberating as laughter, the wild and untamed joy of the animal within.

The Pantomime, the Commedia dell'Arte, the Mummers' Play, the Morris dance, and the music hall were all continuations of this anarchic spirit. As Glyn Hughes demonstrates in his book, "The Antique Collector", the music hall was a place which nurtured freedom of sexuality, as the gay hero of the book discovers. The reversal of the order of things has always been part of the path of self-discovery; the shock of the paradoxical and the mirror-image is an initiatory experience, as anyone who has read "Alice in Wonderland" and "Alice Through the Looking-Glass" will know.

Yule carols

Here is my alternative version of "The Holly and the Ivy":

> The holly and the ivy
> When they are both full grown
> Of all the trees that are in the wood
> The holly bears the crown.
>
> CHORUS: Oh the rising of the sun,
> The running of the deer,
> The Harvest Bride shall be brought to bed,
> And we shall have good cheer.
>
> The holly bears a blossom
> As white as winter snow
> And the Child of Light is newly born
> All on a winter's morn.
>
> The holly bears a prickle
> As sharp as any thorn
> And it has vanquished Barleycorn
> Who sleepeth in the earth.

The holly bears a berry
As red as any wine
And we shall dance and feast all night
In honour of the vine.

And the holly bears a bark
Which burneth with a smoke
And the stag runs in the greenwood
With the lady of the dark.

Another carol with Pagan overtones is Robert Herrick's
"Ceremonies for Christmasse":

Come bring with a noise
My merrie merrie boyes
The Christmas log to the firing
While my good dame, she
Bids ye all be free
And drink to your heart's desiring.

With the last yeeres brand
Light the new block, and
For good success in his spending,
On your Psaltries play,
That sweet luck may
Come while the log is a-tending.

Drink now the strong Beere,
Cut the white loafe here,
The while the meat is a shredding
For the rare Mince-Pie;
And the Plums stand by
To fill the Paste that's a kneading.

Many other alternative folksongs, carols, etc., can be gleaned from the following works:

"Where is Saint George? Pagan imagery in English folksong", by Bob Stewart (Blandford Press, 1988)

"Who Really Killed Cock Robin?" by Norman Iles (Robert Hale, London, 1986)

"Earth, Air, Fire, and Water: Pre-Christian and Pagan Elements in British Songs, Rhymes, and Ballads", by Robin Skelton and Margaret Blackwood (Arkana, London, 1990)

"English and Scottish Ballads" edited by Robert Graves (Poetry Bookshelf, Heinemann, London, 1977)

Yule Customs

The Yule Log: The Yule Log was the sacred wood which, being burnt in the fire, ensured the continuity of the hearth fire, as the fire was transferred from 'last yeeres brand' (which was kept in the house all year round as a charm against fire and lightning). It embodied the vegetation spirit and ensured fertility. Sometimes the log would be brought in with a girl enthroned on it, and glasses were raised to her health. Sometimes corn would be sprinkled on the log, or it would be decorated with Yuletide greenery. In Devon and Cornwall an ashen faggot (a bundle of green ash sticks) would be brought into the pub with three bands tied round it; as each one of these snapped in the fire, the landlord would stand a round of drinks. The log would be chosen and cut beforehand; it must not be bought, but should be got from the householder's land, found elsewhere, or given In Scotland it was oak; in England it was the wood of a fruit tree, or it was ash, the wood of the World Tree. It had to burn continuously for at least twelve hours; in former times, when fireplaces were larger and whole tree trunks were used, it was kept alight for the whole Twelve Days of Christmas. Nor should it be allowed to go out until it was deliberately put out, or it would mean a year's bad luck.

The Christmas tree: The Christmas tree is of course a Pagan custom, and although it was imported from Germany by Prince Albert in the nineteenth century, it is now a part of our tradition. The tree represents the World Tree, Yggdrasil; the baubles are the myriad Worlds, the tinsel is the Rainbow Bridge, or Bifrost, and the custom of bringing the tree indoors represents the perpetuation of the sun's fire at the ebb-tide of the year. The Romans celebrated Saturnalia by decorating a pine tree with little masks of Bacchus.

Mistletoe: Mistletoe, another plant of the sun, was believed to grow where oak trees had been struck by lightning. Hence it was an emanation of the sun's fire, and bestowed fertility and blessing upon the house. In Wiltshire, it is the custom that, every time a couple kiss under the mistletoe, one berry is removed, and when all the berries are gone, the mistletoe must be replaced. Surely there can be no more direct reference to the berries being the semen of the sky-god than this - the god's fertility is directly transferred to the couple by the donation of his seed! And when all the berries are gone, the mistletoe's fertility is exhausted. In many places (notably Brakspear's Brewery at Henley-on-Thames) the mistletoe and holly were kept hanging up all year, to ward off lightning and to ensure a continuous supply of bread. In other places, it was unlucky to keep them hanging up after Twelfth Night, or occasionally, Candlemas.

Pantomime: The enactment of a hero's or heroine's journey, transporting the audience into the world of make-believe, is as old as the hills. As outlined above, the purpose of this journey is twofold: to reverse the normal order of things, breaking down restrictive thought patterns; and to enable the transformation of the audience by giving them an alternative narrative to live by. Pantomime is the whimsical heir to the mystery tradition, whose creed is gleeful subversiveness.

The Mummers' Play: This was a forerunner of the pantomime, closely related in spirit to the Morris and the Commedia dell'Arte. The narrative of the Mummer's Play consisted of the taunting of a King by a Fool, followed by the killing of the Fool by the followers of the King. They then feel ashamed of their action, and call for a doctor to revive the Fool. A doctor (perhaps originally a shaman or druid) appears, and revives the Fool. In some versions the King and the Fool are rivals for the hand of a Lady (clearly the Goddess). The whole narrative appears to be a fertility rite enacting the death and resurrection of the sun, which is reborn at the winter solstice. The origin of the word Mumming may be the Germanic "mummen" (a mask) or the French "momer" (to act in a dumb show).

Fertility Charm (West Midlands): 1st January

On New Year's morning in the West Midlands, the women would bake a hawthorn globe in the oven, which would be hung in the kitchen till the following year. Whilst the new globe was being made, the men set the old one alight and carried it over the newly-sown wheat, letting smouldering twigs fall into every furrow. During the burning they sang a song called "Old Cider" and drank plenty of cider.

Goddess festival (Guatemalan): 1st January

On New Year's Day the Chorti of Southern Guatemala drink the water from five sacred coconuts and fertilise the ground with it. Women officiate at the ceremony, guarding the coconuts in the night and dedicating them to the Goddess before their contents are drunk.

The Haxey Hood Game (Haxey, Lincolnshire): 6th January

Presiding over the game are the Fool, with a blackened face, red shirt, and colourful patched trousers; the Lord of the Hood, with a scarlet hunting coat, a flower-decked top hat, and a wand of thirteen willow rods bound round thirteen times. The proceedings are enlivened by the Boggans, young men in red football shirts, and after the opening ceremonies, participants compete for the Hood in a very rough form of football. The game ends when the Hood reaches either the King's Arms at Haxey or the Carpenter's Arms at Westwoodside.

Wassailing (British): 13th January

> Here's to the old apple tree,
> Whence thou mayest bud, and whence thou mayest blow,
> And whence thou mayest bear apples enow!
> Hats full! Caps full!
> Bushel, bushel sacks full!
> Any my pockets full! Wassail!

The wassailers poured cider over the roots of the tree, hit it with sticks, and fired shots into the air. In some places, people would dip a piece of toast in cider to eat at the wassailing, leaving a piece in the branches for the robins. Wassailing generally occurred on January 5th, 13th, or 17th. The wassailing bowls used to pour the libation were made from maplin (maple wood).

Worcestershire St. Thomas's Day Song

Wassail, wassail, all over the town,
Our toast is white, our ale is brown,
Our bowl is made of a maplin tree;
We be good fellows all - I drink to Thee!

Early 17th c. wassail bowl recipe: "Boil three pints of ale; beat six eggs, the whites and yolks together; set both to the fire in a pewter pot; add roasted apples. honey, beaten nutmegs, clover, and ginger; and being well brewed, drink it hot." (N.B. Eggs may be omitted and cider substituted for beer.)

The aim of wassailing was to make the apple trees bear a lot of fruit, by stirring them up and waking them from their winter sleep.

Wassailing is still done at Carhampton in Somerset (17th January or Old Twelfth Night) and at Henfield in West Sussex (6th January or New Twelfth Night). At Carhampton they sing their wassailing song and then fire shotguns through the branches of the trees ('to scare off evil spirits') and the trees' health is drunk in warm cider on which pieces of toast are floated. Some of this is poured on the roots, and pieces of the toast are left in the branches. At Henfield the ceremony (a revival) is called Apple Howling, and the ceremony includes the blowing of horns and the thrashing of the tree 'to make him bear'.

Carhampton Wassail Song

Old apple tree, we wassail thee, and hoping thou wilt
    bear
For the Lord doth know where we shall be, till apples
    come another year,
To bear well and bloom well so merry let us be

Let every man take off his hat and shout to the old apple
　　tree
Old apple tree, we wassail thee, and hoping thou wilt
　　bear
Hat-fulls, cap-fulls, three-bushel bagfulls
And a little heap under the stairs
Hip! Hip! Hooray!

Henfield Wassail Song (Apple Howling)

Stand fast root, bear well top
God send us a good howling crop
Every twig, apples big! Every bough, apples enow!

(This is followed by a final chorus of howls, 'to wake him up'.)

The custom of wassailing is also being revived by Pagans with
apple-trees. It can be done for other fruit-trees as well.

Imbolc, Candlemas, or Brigantia: 2nd February

Traditionally this is the festival of fire, healing and poetry.
This fits in very well with the mythos of the tree, because the
springing of the fire from the wood is the birth of the god from
the mother, which is the tree. Like the phoenix, the wood is
consumed in the fire, but its energy is released in a new form.
In the Song of Amergin, the bard invokes the "god who sets
the head afire with smoke" who "knows the secrets of the
unhewn dolmen". This is the god who springs from the wood,
the consuming fire of inspiration. The festival of Imbolc is in
honour of Brighid, who is a goddess of fire, poetry, and
healing. Imbolc celebrates intoxication, inspiration, and new
growth. The red colour of the trees' new growth is a living
embodiment of the fire springing from the wood.

140

In terms of the vegetation cycle, Imbolc is the putting forth of the shoot from the seed. In psychological terms, it is the burst of creativity following the experience of spiritual rebirth.

Imbolc Customs

The Biddy: In Ireland it is traditional to bring a representation of Brighid into the house, known as a Biddy. The doll, made of reeds or corn stalks, is laid side by side with a phallic club representing the god. This symbolises the return of fertility to the land, banishing winter and welcoming in the spring.

Scrying: As this is a time of inspiration, it is usual to practice some form of divination. Fire-scrying would perhaps be the most appropriate form of divination. All that is involved is simply gazing into a fire, which induces a state of trance where visions float into the awareness. It is similar to crystal-gazing or water-scrying.

Holly Boy and Ivy Girl (East Kent): Tuesday before Shrove Tuesday

In an obscure village in Kent in 1779, the girls of the village (aged from 5 to 18) were observed burning the effigy of a Holly Boy, which they had stolen from the boys, while in another part of the village, the boys were burning an effigy of the Ivy Girl, which they had stolen from the girls. The whole ceremony was carried out with a lot of shouting.

Kalends of March (Roman): 1st March

This day was sacred to Mars, as was the whole month of March. The sacred fire in the shrine of Vesta was relit on 1st

March, and priests' home and other sacred buildings were decorated with fresh laurel branches (sacred to Mars).

Festival of Iduna (Norse): 3rd March

The Norse goddess Iduna was the keeper of the golden apples, the food of the gods and goddesses of Asgard which kept them immortal and ever-young. Apples are generally regarded as the food of the Otherworld in folklore, myth, and fairytale. Iduna is the wife of Bragi, god of poetry and boasting (in ancient times it was one of the functions of the bard to compose lengthy odes on the prowess and genealogy of the chieftain).

Festival of Artemis (Greek): 21st March

At Athens the festival of Artemis as goddess of game and hunting was celebrated with offerings of cakes in the shape of deer.

Eostre or Spring Equinox: 21st March

This is the festival of Ostara or Eostre, goddess of Spring, the Moon, and hares. It is the midpoint of the Waxing Year, when day and night are equal, but day has the ascendancy. In heathen Scotland it was the feast of Frigga.

In Ancient Egypt it was a festival of Isis, celebrating the return of the waters of the Nile and the first green shoots in the fields.

In Greece the return of Persephone from Hades was celebrated; she is depicted on many Greek vases rising from a mound, which is sometimes surmounted by a tree.

In terms of the vegetation cycle the equinox is the appearance of the shoot above the earth, and the putting forth of leaves by the mature plant. Psychologically, it is the reconciliation of opposites.

Spring Equinox is the festival of the earth goddess, giver of life. She has been represented from time immemorial as the tree from whom the young god springs, in the form of fire. She is the tree of life, which many cultures have seen as emerging from the world egg.

Eostre Customs

"Pussy Willow": Pagan spring festivals in honour of Freyja included the use of the "Pussy Willow", the Great Sallow or Goat Willow (Salix caprea), which is still used to decorate churches on Palm Sunday. Freyja's totem animal was the cat, hence perhaps the name "Pussy Willow".

Pace Eggs: In many parts of England and Scotland, it was customary to make Pace Eggs at Easter. These were hard-boiled eggs which were wrapped in onion-skin to dye them in beautiful marbled patterns. The method is to wrap the onion-skin around the egg and secure it with cotton thread, then to boil it in a pan for 15 minutes. When the egg is cool, the onion skin is removed, leaving the marbled pattern on the egg-shell. The Pace Egg was then rolled downhill in a contest to see whose egg reached the bottom of the hill first.

Painted Eggs: In Europe, painted eggs were given as gifts at Easter, or hidden around the house and garden for the children to find.

Chocolate Eggs: The custom of giving chocolate eggs at Easter is derived from the older tradition of painted eggs. The egg is a symbol of rebirth, fertility, and creation. It was used in many fertility customs, associated with both sowing and harvest.

Easter Bonnets: The wearing of Easter Bonnets may derive from some older tradition of dressing up as the vegetation spirit, since the bonnet consists of flowers, fruit, and other Easter symbols.

The "Easter Bunny": The "Easter Bunny" is of course Ostara's hare, the moon animal par excellence. The mad March hare is stirred by the renewal of the tides of life to dancing and boxing and mating in the fields. The hare is the messenger of the moon, and hence also of the unconscious. Witches were said to shape-shift into hares.

Hot Cross Buns: These were a relic of the pagan moon-cakes. Also, the equal-armed cross scored on the hot-cross bun could be taken to represent the sacred circle of the four quarters, the four cardinal directions, and the four solar festivals of the year. The Greeks offered horned cakes to Apollo, Diana, Hecate, and the Moon; the 'cross' symbolised the four phases of the moon. In Hertfordshire, where the Icknield Way crosses Ermine Street, there was an altar to Diana of the Crossways; the neighbourhood has always been famous for its hot cross buns.

Wassailing: Before the calendar reform of 1752, the year began in England on 25th March, and the New Year's Day custom of wassailing occurred then. In Scotland the New Year was moved to 1st January around 1600. As the death and resurrection of many Dying Gods (representing the vegetation spirit) was celebrated at the Spring Equinox, this fertility charm for the renewal of life is quite apt for this time of year also.

Gardens of Adonis: These were baskets or pots filled with earth, in which wheat, barley, lettuces, fennel, and various flowers were sown and tended for eight days, mostly by women. The custom survives in Sicily, and was observed on Maundy Thursday at Hammersmith in London in 1944, where little gardens had been planted on the pavement, each planted with twelve tiny shoots of privet and protected with branches. This was a custom transferred from the Pagan worship of Adonis to the worship of Christ.

Palilia or Parilia (Roman): 21st April

The Palilia is the festival of Pales. This deity is so ancient that it is now unclear whether it is a goddess or a god, or even a divine couple. Most writers seem to incline to the view that it is a goddess. Pales was the deity of flocks. At her festival, houses were decorated with greenery, sheepfolds were festooned with boughs, and people made a large bonfire of beanstraw and laurel. An offering of dried blood and sacrificial ashes was thrown onto the fire, and an offering of cakes and milk was made to Pales. Prayers were said, then all present sprinkled their hands with holy water from a laurel branch, and jumped three times through the flames. This festival evolved from a purely pastoral occasion into a national and urban celebration, said to be the day on which the building of Rome was begun.

St. George's Day (British and European): 23rd April

St. George is an embodiment of the vegetation spirit, who returns to life after the winter when the leaves begin to appear on the trees. His slaying of the dragon represents the triumph of creation over formless chaos, and triumphing over the dragon or serpent which guards the tree of life. The rescue of the maiden symbolises the sacred marriage with the anima.

In Russia and other Slavic countries the personification of the vegetation spirit is called Green George, a leaf-clad youth appearing on St. George's Day (23rd April) bearing gifts and followed by girls singing. This custom is also prevalent among Hungarian Gypsies.

Ludi Florae (Roman): 27th April - 3rd May

The Games of Flora lasted for six days. They began with theatrical performances, and ended with circus games and a sacrifice to Flora. The Floralia festival was celebrated on 3rd May. Flora was the ancient Italian goddess of flowers, vegetation, and fruit trees, hence also fertility. As a result of this aspect, much licentious behaviour prevailed on her festival. Originally this was of a rustic character, but later it took on a more urban aspect. Prostitutes claimed both the Floralia and the Vinalia (23rd April) as their feast. Roman youth went en masse into the fields and danced and sang in honour of Flora; Roman children made little images of Flora and decorated them with flowers.

Beltane: 30th April / 1st May

The festival of Beltane or May Eve was traditionally associated with Robin Hood and Maid Marian, and also featured the Maypole, the May Queen, and/or the May King.

Robin Hood may have been a real person, or more than one person; certainly the archetype of the forest outlaw is very ancient. Robin Hood is the lord of the forest, the wild and untameable one. His consort Marian represents the Goddess, and their union is a symbol of fertility, the renewal of the land. Marian appears to have taken on some of the attributes of Flora (in whose honour the Romans celebrated Floralia on 1st May). Robin Hood represents the archetype of the divine archer, the god of hunting; he appears to have taken on some aspects of Odin (who is the leader of the Wild Hunt in Germanic folklore), and is also associated with Herne, the horned stag god of the forests (leader of the Wild Hunt in English folklore). For an in-depth study of this subject, "Robin Hood: The Spirit of the Forest" by Steve Wilson (Neptune Press, 1993) is highly recommended reading.

Morris dancing is also closely associated with the May festivities, and with Robin Hood and his Merrie Men. Morris dancing was a tradition brought from Spain which appears to have been grafted onto an earlier form of fertility dance. One such form was Contray Dancing (contray was a Norman French word meaning opposite), where lines of women danced opposite lines of men. Morris dancing before the Interregnum included women, and many Morris sides had character parts (Robin Hood, Maid Marian, Friar Tuck, Will Scarlet, Little John, etc., with Much the Miller's Son as the Fool). When it was revived after the Restoration, this aspect seems to have been forgotten, and most sides were men only, though other traditional dances included women (e.g. Molly Dancing). A stained-glass window at Betley in Staffordshire depicts twelve Morris dancers, including Robin Hood as the May King, Maid Marian with a golden crown, holding a summer pink, Friar Tuck with a ring of bells, a hobby horse with a ladle for donations, a piper with a tabor, a Fool with a bauble, a coxcomb hood, and ass ears, and six Morris dancers with bells at their knees.

The maypole is the axis mundi around which the universe revolves. The tree, stripped of its foliage which symbolises change, becomes the changeless axis or centre. The pole itself is phallic; the discus at the top from which the ribbons are suspended represents the feminine principle; the union of the two in the maypole represents fertility. The seven ribbons are the colours of the rainbow.

Originally the maypole was the sacred pine of Attis which was taken in procession or on a chariot to the temple of Cybele, where it was set up to be venerated. It was followed in the procession by men, women, and children, and dances were held round it.

Later this ceremony appeared in the Roman Hilaria, the Spring Festival, and then in the May Day celebrations of the May Queen and the Green Man, the spirit of vegetation.The ribbons of the maypole possibly derive from the bands of wool wrapped round the Attis pine. The entire ceremony is symbolic of renewed life, sexual union, resurrection, and spring.

In Sweden the maypole is erected on Midsummer's Eve; elsewhere it is erected on May Eve or Beltane (31st April). In Cornwall and Northamptonshire it was the custom to erect a may tree outside every house, and to deck the porches with hawthorn and sycamore. In Germany the maypole is generally a tall pine stripped of its branches; in Sweden it is a spruce; everywhere it is decked with ribbons, flowers, painted eggshells, and bunting. In 1583 the Puritan writer Philip Stubbes railed against the bringing in of the maypole from the woods, accompanied by much mirth and revelry. The overnight ceremonies in the wood involved the celebration of the union of the Goddess and the God; children born of these couplings were known as merrybegots, and held to partake of the divine nature which overshadowed their parents at the time of conception.

In some parts of Europe, young men would erect a may tree outside the home of their sweetheart. Dancing around the pole was almost universal; in some places there was a race on foot or on horseback to the foot of the maypole. In all these cases the custom was to bring in a new maypole every year. This has lapsed in some places, where a permanent maypole has been erected, but there is little doubt that the original practice was to bring in a new pole every year, representing that year's incarnation of the vegetation spirit.

In parts of Russia the old maypole was thrown into the river after three days, perhaps as a rain charm; in many places the old tree was burnt after a year; just as many people keep their palm crosses from Palm Sunday for a year and then burn them. In many places a person or effigy is regarded as the embodiment of the May alongside the may tree or pole. Sometimes there is a May King, more often a May Queen, sometimes a bridegroom and bride. In Scotland it is still the custom for people to wash their faces in the dew on May morning.

At Thann, in Alsace, a girl called the Little May Rose, dressed in white, carries a small may-tree decked with garlands and ribbons. Her companions collect gifts from door to door, and sing:

> Little May Rose turn round three times,
> Let us look at you round and round!
> Rose of the May, come to the greenwood away,
> We will be merry all.
> So we go from the May to the Roses.

The produce of the year depends on giving to the May singers, for the song continues, expressing a wish that those who give nothing will have their fowls eaten by martens, their vines will not bear, their trees will bear no nuts, and their fields no corn.

In Rutland and Norfolk, two intersecting hoops of flowers and evergreens were fixed to the top of a staff and carried round the town accompanied by hooting on cows' horns. Sometimes a doll was fixed to the top of the staff in the centre of the globe formed by the intersecting hoops.

In various parts of the country, it was the custom to blow horns and make a lot of noise with pots and pans, both on May Eve and May Morning.

The Beltane fire was also widespread. Bonfires were a fertility custom, for example burning straw houses or effigies to ensure an abundant harvest, and to keep mildew, blight, and hail from the crops. The custom was observed all over Europe in various forms. In Wales 3 or 9 different kinds of wood and charred faggots from the previous year's bonfire were used. The fire was generally lit on rising ground. Amongst witches it is the custom to leap over the Bel-fire at Beltane; couples leap it hand in hand.

In terms of the vegetation cycle, Beltane represents mystical union, when the plant is in full growth in harmony with its environment. In human terms, it is the time for lovers; but folklore warns (and experience confirms) that love affairs begun in May will only last the summer. Hence it is believed to be unlucky to bring hawthorn boughs (may blossom) into the house except at Beltane, as the blessing they confer is not on long-term relationships.

Various actions were taboo in Ireland on May Day: "Neither fire, nor water, nor milk, nor salt, should be given away for love or money." ('Speranza' Wilde, 1887)

Festival of Maia (Roman): 1st May

The goddess Maia was the mother of Mercury and the consort of Vulcan. She was one of the Pleiades, and the Romans identified her with an old Italian goddess of Spring. The priest of Vulcan (flamen Volcanalis) made an offering to her on 1st May.

Oak Apple Day (English): 29th May

Oak Apple Day was introduced after the Restoration (1660) to commemorate the escape of King Charles II from the Parliamentary forces by hiding in an oak tree at Boscobel in Shropshire after the battle of Worcester (3rd September 1651). An oak leaf was worn, and oak trees dressed, to commemorate this event. Any who neglected to wear an oak leaf were taunted, or, in some places, stung with a nettle held with a dock leaf. 29th May was Charles II's birthday and the day of his public re-entry into London. In some places, a man representing Cromwell, his face smeared with soot, was led through the village on a halter, and would try to catch small boys and smear them with soot. He was followed by a group of men carrying a litter of oak boughs containing a small child, symbolising the renewal brought about by the king's return. Students of folklore will recognise echoes of the theme of the Holly King and the Oak King, the triumph of the hero of light over his dark adversary. The story also contains strong echoes of the "rightful king hiding in the greenwood until the time comes to overthrow the usurper" theme (the same tale is told of Odin, King Horn, Richard the Lionheart, etc.)

Midsummer

The Summer Solstice (21st June) or Midsummer (24th June) have long been celebrated over a wide area. Many places would roll a burning cartwheel downhill, symbolising vividly the descent of the sun into the underworld.

The most ancient sun deities in the Northern Tradition were female. It is widely believed that Freyja was a sun goddess. Prudence Jones has suggested that the amber necklace Brisingamen is the rising and setting of the sun as it moves round the horizon during the year, and the four dwarves with whom Freyja has sex are the four cardinal directions, at which the sun rises and sets at the solstices and equinoxes.

It is possible that St. Catherine, with her attribute of a burning wheel, is a Christianisation of a Pagan sun goddess. The hill next to Twyford Down (near Winchester) is called St. Catherine's Hill, and there is a maze on top of it.

Midsummer is the culmination of the sun's power, the longest day and the shortest night. Psychologically it represents the turning point from waxing strength to waning strength. In terms of the vegetation cycle, it is the point at which the flower is fertilised, and begins to be transformed into fruit. Maximum growth has been achieved, and the plant must put its energy into producing seed for the perpetuation of the species.

Midsummer Customs and Beliefs

Midsummer's Eve was believed to be a night when the faeries were abroad. Accordingly, country folk took precautions against their cattle being stolen away. Rowan and birch twigs were used for protection; some farmers made passes over their cattle with a lighted branch. Also, rowan twigs were tucked into horses' bridles, and tied to cows' tails with red thread.

In the Christian calendar, Midsummer is St. John's Day, and the plant St. John's Wort (Hypericum perforatum), which flowers around this time, is the flower of Midsummer. Its name Hypericum, according to Mrs. Grieve, is derived from the Greek and means 'over an apparition', referring to the belief that the plant could ward off evil spirits. It also has medicinal uses, and is aromatic, astringent, and balsamic. According to Culpeper it is ruled by the Sun and is under the sign of Leo.

Mazes were also a feature of Midsummer festivities; the maze at Saffron Walden was used for races until fairly recently.

Mazes were known as Troy Town, which was derived from the Celtic 'Caer Droia', meaning the place of turning. The symbolism of the maze is similar to that of the Castle of Arianrhod, which is mythically located at the Pole Star, traditionally known as the Nowl or God's Nail.

A vestige of the Midsummer bonfire still survives at Whalton in Northumberland, where the Baal Fire (a corruption of Celtic 'Bel', meaning bright) used to burn on 4th July (Old Midsummer Eve). Now the custom has dwindled to toasting the Baal at the village pub, and distributing sweets to children. In its heyday, couples used to jump through the embers 'for luck', and the gorse which was burnt could only be hauled by horse and cart as far as the village boundary. After that it had to be hauled into the village by hand, with much shouting and blowing of horns. Before it was lit, children would join hands and dance round it, and then scramble for sweets and pennies.

Festival of Ishtar and Tammuz (Mesopotamian): 23rd June

The death and resurrection of the Dying God (the vegetation spirit) was originally celebrated in the Middle East at midsummer, when Sirius rose in Leo after a disappearance of seventy days.

Bawming the Thorn (Appleton Thorn, near Warrington, Cheshire): late June

Originally held on 29th June (St. Peter's Day), this is a custom of embalming or adorning a tree which grew from a sliver of the Glastonbury Thorn, brought to Cheshire by a 12th-century Lord of the manor, Adam de Dutton. The present tree was planted in 1967, as a replacement of its predecessor, which was a descendant of the original tree. The original festivities were rather rowdy, and were discontinued in Victorian times; the custom was briefly revived in the 1930s, and is now celebrated by local children. Originally it was performed mainly by unmarried girls, so this is quite apt.

Sothis (Egyptian): 19th July

In Egypt, the rising of Sirius coincided with the rising of the waters of the Nile, which symbolised the resurrection of Osiris. The Egyptians called the star Sothis, whilst the constellation of Orion (which the Dog Star follows) was called Osiris. Sothis represented the dog Anubis.

Lammas / Lughnassad: July 31st / August 1st

Lammas is primarily a harvest festival linked to the mysteries of John Barleycorn. It was also a time for handfastings, 'trial marriages' which continued for a year and a day, and which could be proclaimed to be permanent at the following Lammas. It was a time for promises and pledges. It is generally the time for mourning the death of the sun god; in Lancashire the first week of August was called the Wakes. In terms of the vegetation cycle, it is the time when the cycle is completed; the plant has produced seed, the fruit are ripening, and the cycle is ready to begin again. In Ireland it is called Lughnasadh.

Woodmen of Arden's Grand Wardmote (Meriden, Warwickshire): first week in August

The Woodmen of Arden are a company of eighty archers founded in 1785, based on the medieval bands of bowmen. The village of Meriden is said to be at the exact centre of England,

154

and to have been the site of an archery contest attended by Robin Hood. The Grand Wardmote is a four-day archery contest, in which contestants use six-foot yew bows of medieval pattern, but their costume is eighteenth century; they wear a green frock-coat and buff waistcoat with gilt buttons, a broad-brimmed green shooting hat, and white trousers.

Festival of Diana (Roman): August 13th

On this day in Rome, hunting dogs were crowned and wild beasts not molested; young people were purified in Diana's honour; and a feast was eaten, with a kid, cakes served hot on plates of leaves, and apples still hanging on the bough.

Festival of Vertumnus (Roman): August 13th

Two of the rustic deities of the ancient Roman pantheon were Pomona and Vortumnus (or Vertumnus). Pomona is the protectress of fruits, associated with Flora and Ceres. She is the lady of the fields and orchards. She brings water in trickling streams for the twining roots to drink; she trains the vines and prunes the trees; she tends the savoury garden herbs. The first one to taste of her fruits is Vortumnus, whose wild autumnal winds transform the land, bringing the snow and the rain. Vortumnus is the god of transformation and the power of cyclical change; his name is derived from the verb 'uorti', to be turned, to be transformed. It is for Vortumnus that the first bunches of grapes turn blue, and for him the ear of grain swells with a milky juice. Here you may see the sweet cherries, the autumnal plums, the mulberries blushing under the summer sun. He is the god of the changing seasons, who can assume any shape. He may have been derived from an Etruscan goddess, Veltune; or his name may be a Latinisation of an Etruscan name. The Romans insisted that he was of

Etruscan origin. Legend has it that Pomona, who was very beautiful, refused all offers of marriage. Eventually Vortumnus managed to see her by disguising himself as an old woman. In this guise he proceeded to tell her how much he loved her, but still it was of no avail. Then he revealed himself to her in all his glory, and she 'was smitten with a passion equal to his own'. (Ovid, "Metamorphoses", XIV.)

Rustic Vinalia (Roman): 19th August

Venus and Minerva were called upon; temples were dedicated to Venus and gardens were set aside for her. There was a holiday for kitchen-gardeners. Olive groves were sacred to Minerva, gardens to Venus.

Autumn Equinox

The Autumn Equinox is the opposite point in the year to the Spring Equinox. Day and night are again equal, but the daylight hours are decreasing as the year moves towards the Winter Solstice.

September is also the month of the fruit harvest, when apples are gathered for cider-making, and many other fruits are ready for picking. In terms of the vegetation cycle, the Autumnal Equinox is when the parent plant produces a seed, bringing its life-cycle to completion. For people, it is a time for preparing for winter, both mentally and physically: jettisoning ideas that have outlived their usefulness; starting new projects; and storing up energy and resources for the winter.

Autumn Equinox Customs

Fruit is picked for wine-making, jam, and preserves. Country tradition has it that blackberries should not be gathered after September 25th, because after that 'the Devil has spat on them'. In other words, it was taboo to gather fruit after the Autumn Equinox.

The Michaelmas Goose: The goose was the sacred bird of Odin, to whom the Autumn Equinox was sacred, and it was eaten at this time of year as a sacral meal. The custom continued into the Christian era under the guise of Michaelmas and Martinmas.

In the west of Scotland and the Hebrides, Michaelmas was celebrated with horse-racing and the giving of gifts, particularly carrots, which were harvested and blessed at Michaelmas. A cake called the Struan Micheil, made from the year's cereals, was baked and eaten.

Crabapple Fair (Egremont, near Whitehaven, Cumbria): 18th October

This fair was established by charter in 1267, and has been held continuously since (apart from the two world wars). It takes its name from the custom of distributing free apples, nowadays from a lorry which tours the village shortly after noon. Originally the crab apples were used as ammunition in a fight. Other activities include climbing a greasy pole, Cumberland wrestling, and 'gurning through a braffin' (pulling faces through a horse collar).

Chapter 5

Working magically with trees

> Choose the willow of the streams,
> Choose the hazel of the rocks,
> Choose the alder of the marshes,
> Choose the birch of the waterfalls.
>
> Choose the ash of the shade,
> Choose the yew of resilience,
> Choose the elm of the brae,
> Choose the oak of the sun.
>
> ("Choice of timber" from the Carmina Gadelica)

Everything is interdependent, but meanings shift and evolve. The patterns in the collective unconscious are continuously changing and growing, stretching and shrinking, as new experiences are integrated, and old ones fade from view. Symbolism is not fixed; there is no 'correct version' of anything. For a tradition to survive, it must evolve and include new insights and methods of working. Magic is a way of seeing the world which is different from the materialist view which is prevalent in our culture. (By materialist I mean believing only in material reality.) The unseen, whether it be metaphorical or spiritual, is consistently undervalued in our culture.

We are taught to regard intuition as unreliable; hence many people are searching for some 'authentic' magical tradition, handed down in an unbroken line over the centuries. They are unlikely to succeed in finding much; genuine hereditary traditions are rare. But the criterion of authenticity is not necessarily antiquity; an authentic spirituality can arise as the result of intuitive insights into the nature of things. We must learn to trust our intuition, and celebrate the many different approaches to pagan spirituality.

Magic, and its related arts, poetry and music, are open to individual interpretation. The medium in which the artist works (the unseen in the case of magic, language for poetry, and the range of audible notes in music) is the same for every practitioner of the art, but what an enormous range of individual interpretation is possible within that medium. What characterises a magician, a poet, or a musician, is that they are viewing and interpreting the world in a different way, which is by its very nature idiosyncratic. All these arts are based on metaphor, which is seldom recognised as an occult art.

Metaphor is a fundamental part of our cognitive processes, and affects the way in which we view the world. We use metaphor and analogical thinking as an aid to understanding new situations, which we compare with previous experiences. Metaphors vary considerably from one culture to another, as does magical symbolism. It has been suggested that the use of metaphor in language is derived from sympathetic magic and totemic social structures (Wicker, 1975). Those who could use language and sound creatively were recognised as people who could transform consciousness (in other words, magicians or shamans). It is not for nothing that Woden is the god of both poetry and magic; the inspired fury of creativity belongs to both these arts.

According to J. G. Frazer, sympathetic magic can be subdivided into two categories: homeopathic magic (the law of similarity) and contagious magic (the law of contact). Homeopathic magic is born of the idea that like begets like; if you perform an action on an object which represents something, the thing represented will be affected accordingly. Contagious magic is the use of a magically charged thing directly on the person or thing one is desirous of affecting; an obvious example here would be a talisman. Many forms of spell conflate the two types of magic.

Many people are sceptical of the existence of magic, but if, as some philosophers and physicists believe, reality can be affected by the observer, then a change in the consciousness of the observer will bring about a change in reality. Hence Aleister Crowley's definition of magic: changing consciousness in conformity with Will (i.e. the higher self, the part of us which is godhead made manifest). The symbolic correspondences provide a language to bring about this change in consciousness, invoking the archetypes associated with the desired effect. For example, the apple is ruled by Venus, so it is commonly used in love spells. However, in Celtic symbolism, it is a fruit of the underworld, so it is also eaten at Samhain to symbolise this.

There are three levels of symbolism, according to Jung. There is personal symbolism, which varies from one individual to another (e.g. a certain flower reminds you of your mother). There is cultural symbolism, which is common to a group of people (e.g. the motorbike symbolises freedom to Hell's Angels). Then there are the underlying archetypes, which are common to humanity, but which are expressed slightly differently in different cultures (e.g. the goddess of love, who has been represented as Ishtar, Venus, Aphrodite, etc.).

So magic is not a closed system, but is open to creative insights. Some people may feel that the Elm tree corresponds to the element of Earth, others may feel that it corresponds to Water. Whichever attribution fits in best with your personal view is true for you. As you will have noticed by now if you have read more than one book on magic, one person will say that the rune Isa is black, another will say it is white. Both attributions are valid, because they are based on personal experience with the Runes.

The important thing in magic is to follow your own instinct. Learn as many different ways of doing things as you like, but think about what you are doing and why you are doing it. A simple example of this is sweeping a circle before beginning a working. If you do this, do you do it to sweep luck in, to cleanse the area of negativity, or both? Or are you just doing it because it said in the book that you should? Your answer to this will determine how you actually sweep. If you are doing it to sweep luck in, you will probably sweep towards the centre of the circle; if you are cleansing the area, you will probably sweep away from the centre. If you are doing it because the book told you to, you will probably wave the broom around the edge of the circle a bit, looking sheepish. But when you are sweeping actual physical dirt on your kitchen floor, what do you do? You sweep all the dirt into a heap, then brush it out of the door. Similarly, when sweeping the circle, you do not want all the dirt hanging around at the edge of the circle, ready to creep back in when the ritual is over. Another thing: do you sweep widdershins to banish negativity, or deosil to bring in positive energies? The answer is up to you. As long as there is a reason behind what you do, your magic will probably work. If you analyse everything you do in this way, you will no longer be just going through the motions of a ritual. Everything will feel right and fit logically with what you are doing. Examine in particular all those things that you take for granted. For example, is the use of the pentagram appropriate to your working? Are you comfortable with metal working tools? When should you move deosil, and when is moving widdershins permissible? And so on. Do not just take someone else's word for it, try it for yourself. Be prepared to learn from others, but do not regard tradition as graven on tablets of stone.

TREES IN RITUAL

Trees are living entities, and as such, should be treated with respect. Before taking anything from a tree (branch, twig, leaf, or bark), it is necessary to ask the tree's permission. It is even better if you leave some kind of gift for the tree (preferably something of practical use like clearing the site of litter).

Making wands, staffs, brooms, and stangs

The art of making a wand is very subtle. The first stage is to find a suitable piece of wood. If you walk around a forest on a number of different occasions, getting to know its moods and the different trees that grow there, and making friends with the spirit of place, you may eventually be honoured with the gift of a piece of wood. My favourite wand is a piece of beech which I found lying around in the New Forest, Hampshire, which is gnarled in such a way that one end looks like a goat's head, and the other resembles the female genitalia. When you find something like this, it is obvious that it does not need carving. All it needs is a bit of tender loving care.

If you have a more conventionally wand-shaped piece of wood which you propose to carve, try and communicate with it to find out if it wants to be carved. If you do this, it will co-operate in the process. Some pieces of wood seem to be faintly embarrassed at being carved into a phallic shape; other bits of wood seem to love the idea, and emerge from the carving process positively glowing with masculine energy; some trees deliberately grow in that shape (especially beech trees). Some woods will not mind having their bark removed, others will not like it. Some will just want polishing with fragrant oils, others may be varnished. The important thing to remember is to treat it with respect. You are not imposing a shape on it, you are bringing out a shape that was inherent in the wood. I have a piece of driftwood which looks like a fox; all that needed to be done was to remove the sharp edges and polish it with oil. Nature carved it; all I did was to recognise a work of art when I saw it.

The basic things that you will need are: a saw, a knife, some sandpaper (various grades), a workbench, some matt varnish and a brush, or linseed oil and a soft rag, and a peaceful place to work. The piece of wood on which you are working will need to have been seasoned for at least a year (preferably four years), and reasonably free of rot, woodworm, etc. To season your piece of wood, leave it in a dry place with a constant temperature, where it will harden and dry out gradually.

Making a staff or a stang is similar. Obviously the choice of wood is more limited, as it needs to be straight, about the right height, and able to support your weight. As it is longer and thicker than a wand, there is more scope for carving, but again, I feel that carving should be minimal, and carried out in close communication with the wood. As it is a magical tool, it exists in both the physical and the spiritual realms, and should be treated from the start as a friend, not as a servant.

The type of wood you use to make the wand will vary according to your affinity with a particular tree, or with the deities, planet, rune, or ogham associated with that tree, and the type of magic in which the wand will be used. For details of the magical uses of trees, see Appendix Four. Divining rods are usually made of hazel, and hazel wands were used by the druids as a symbol of authority. A blackthorn staff was the witch's symbol of authority. Willow is used for any ritual associated with the Moon. Wands are often tipped with an acorn (symbol of fertility and renewal) or a pine cone (deal apple, symbol of Dionysos); the thyrsus of Dionysiac rites was a staff tipped with a pine cone. The Celtic wand was made of hazel; the Gaelic white wand from yew.

Wassail cups were traditionally made of maplin or maple wood. A recipe for the Wassail Bowl is given in the chapter on seasonal festivals.

Sprite flails (for banishing malign spirits) are made of bramble, because of its qualities of psychic protection and binding.

In the case of the broom or besom, certain woods are traditional. The shaft is made of willow or hazel. Willow is symbolic of purification and rebirth, and is sacred to the Moon and to the goddess Freyja. Hazel represents inspiration and divination, and is sacred to Thor. The thongs are made of ash or willow. Ash is the World Tree in the Northern Tradition, and is sacred to Woden. The besom is made of birch twigs (birth and rebirth), hazel twigs (fire, fertility, poetry, divination, and knowledge), and/or yew twigs (death and resurrection). The handle is the masculine principle, the brush is the feminine principle, which unite to bring about birth (birch twigs). Life is represented by poetry and inspiration (hazel), and initiation (ash). If there is birth, it follows that there must also be death (yew), but there will also be rebirth (yew and birch). The purpose of the broom is purification, which is represented by willow and birch.

In many covens, the hilt of the sword was made of elder because judgement was traditionally given under elder trees.

Consecrating working tools

As a home-made tool has a history known to you, it does not really need to be cleansed. If you have bought a second-hand item, it is usually advisable to cleanse it magically. (In theory, of course, you should never buy a magical tool, but wait until it is given to you.) A home-made tool, however, only really needs to be blessed and dedicated to use in your rituals. Once it has been consecrated, it should not be used for anything which is incompatible with ritual (e.g. you would not use your cauldron as a repository for phone bills and nasty letters from the bank).

The form which the consecration takes varies from one tradition to another, but it is usual to bless and/or purify the tool with incense, water, and salt, to dedicate it for use, and then to use it straight away in your magical working for the purpose for which it is intended.

Using magical tools

The wand is used where it would be inappropriate to use the athame, that is, in dealings with the world of Faerie. The antipathy of the faery folk to iron is well-known. There are various theories to account for this; the most probable one is that iron blocks the flow of life-energy. (This is why the stang was shod with iron in some traditions, so that the magical energy would build up in the stang and not disperse.) The wand may also be used instead of the athame for the consecration of wine. The wand is a conductor of energy, which focuses the energy into a particular thing or place. The stang is used as a representation of the World Tree, to anchor the circle in the centre of the world. It is also used as a focus for magical energies, a totem of the Horned God (hence it is often forked at the top or surmounted by an antler), and a personal staff. The staff is used both as a walking stick and as a large wand.

Various woods are also burnt in the bonfire at festivals. The Nine Woods of the Beltane Fire are: ash, birch, yew, hazel, rowan, willow, pine, and thorn. Oak, however, should not be used, because it is the king of the woods. The woods burnt would probably vary according to local availability, but oak would not have been used, nor alder (sacred to Bran), nor

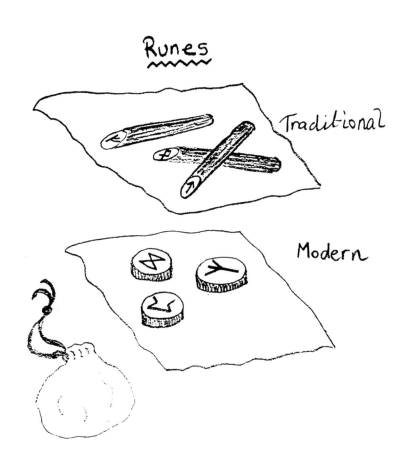

Making your own runes

elder (sacred to Hella, goddess of the Underworld).

The Yule Log, burnt at Yule, was traditionally made of ash. In Devon and Cornwall, it was the custom for the innkeeper to burn one which was bound with three bands; whenever one of them snapped in the fire, a free round of drinks was served.

The seven Chieftain trees of old Irish law, which it was unlawful to fell because they were sacred, were hazel, apple, yew, holly, pine, ash, and oak.

Making Runes

The word Rune comes from the same source as rowan. Related words include the Old English rown, to whisper, and the Gaelic run, a secret. When making runes, some people make them all from the same piece of wood, choosing a wood with which they have have an affinity, making flat coin-shaped pieces. Other people use the more traditional shape, a slender stem with a diagonally cut face on the end, on which the rune is painted or carved. In this case you could use wood from the appropriate tree for each rune (see the section on the Germanic peoples in the chapter on the mysteries of the forest for a list of correspondences). Some practitioners make and energise each rune at the appropriate hour of the day. The runic hours are as follows:

Tide of the day	Rune	Times	Peak time
Noontide	Fehu	12.30 to 13.30	1 p.m.
Undorne	Uruz	13.30 to 14.30	2 p.m.
	Thurisaz	14.30 to 15.30	3 p.m.
	Ansuz	15.30 to 16.30	4 p.m.

Eventide	Raido	16.30 to 17.30	5 p.m.
	Kenaz	17.30 to 18.30	6 p.m.
	Gebo	18.30 to 19.30	7 p.m.
Night-tide	Wunjo	19.30 to 20.30	8 p.m.
	Hagalaz	20.30 to 21.30	9 p.m.
	Nauthiz	21.30 to 22.30	10 p.m.
Midnight	Isa	22.30 to 23.30	1 p.m.
	Jera	23.30 to 00.30	12 p.m.
	Eihwaz	00.30 to 01.30	1 a.m.
Uht	Perth	01.30 to 02.30	2 a.m.
	Algiz	02.30 to 03.30	3 a.m.
	Sowelu	03.30 to 04.30	4 a.m.
Morning	Teiwaz	04.30 to 05.30	5 a.m.
	Berkana	05.30 to 06.30	6 a.m.
	Ehwaz	06.30 to 07.30	7 a.m.
Undernoon	Mannaz	07.30 to 08.30	8 a.m.
	Laguz	08.30 to 09.30	9 a.m.
	Nguz	09.30 to 10.30	10 a.m.
Noontide	Othila	10.30 to 11.30	11 a.m.
	Dagaz	11.30 to 12.30	12 a.m.
	Fehu	12.30 to 13.30	1 p.m.

Remember to convert to Greenwich Mean Time if you are making the runes in Summer, as Noon should be when the Sun is at the meridian. (In British Summer Time, the Sun is at the meridian at 1 p.m.)

Traditional spells using trees

Apple peel: a whole strip of rind pared from an apple was thrown over the shoulder to discover the initial of the future husband's first name.

Burning apple pips: Apple pips were thrown on the fire; if they popped as they burnt, your lover's ardour had not cooled; if they burnt silently, he had lost interest.

"If you love me, pop and fly,
If you hate me, lay and die."

Squeezing apple pips: a pip was shot from between the thumb and forefinger, saying:

"Kernel come kernel, hop over my thumb,
And tell me which way my truelove will come,
East, west, north, or south,
Kernel jump into my truelove's mouth." (Dorset, 1844)

Pressing apple pips to the face: Pips were designated as one or more lovers and pressed to the forehead or cheek. If they fell off, the lover was not true; if they stuck, he was.

Even ash: If you found an ash sprig with an even number of leaves, it was believed that you would get good luck and see your true love before the day was over.

Ash keys: If there were no ash keys, it portended a death in the royal family, or some public calamity. This is interesting in view of the fact that the Anglo-Saxon kings (from whom the present monarch is descended) were believed to be descended from Woden, to whom ash trees are sacred.

Bay leaves: Pinning bay leaves to your pillow, one at each corner and one in the middle (especially on Valentine's Day) was said to make you dream of your sweetheart.

Fruit stones (plums, damsons, cherries): By counting the stones left on your plate, a species of divination was performed to find out your future occupation. Various rhymes were employed, the most common being "Tinker, tailor, soldier, sailor, rich man, poor man, beggarman, thief" and "This year, next year, some time, never". The last stone to be reached was the one which indicated your fate.

Ivy-leaf: Plucking an ivy-leaf unobserved and putting it in your bosom was said to mean that the next man you saw would be your future husband. Placing an ivy-leaf in water overnight on Hallowe'en or over the twelve days of Christmas was said to indicate the state of your health for the coming year. If it remained fresh and green, you would be well; if it became blemished, you would be ill. ·

Mistletoe: When the previous year's mistletoe was burnt (just before the new bunch was put up) the maidens of the parish would watch the fire anxiously: if it spat and crackled, it portended ill-tempered husbands; if it burnt steadily, it was a sign of even-tempered husbands.

Nutmeg: Carrying a nutmeg in your pocket was said to cure backache and lumbago; however, it was also said to mean that you would marry an old man. To cure boils, the sufferer was given a nutmeg by a member of the opposite sex, which was then nibbled at from time to time until it was gone; when the nutmeg had been eaten, the boils would also disappear.

Nuts: A good nut year was said to mean a lot of babies born. In Devon, a bag of nuts was presented to a newlywed bride by an old woman, betokening fruitfulness. Nuts were also burnt in the fire to see how a courtship would progress:

> "Two Hazel-Nuts I threw into the Flame.
> And to each Nut I gave a Sweet-heart's Name.
> This with the loudest Bounce me sore amaz'd,
> That in a Flame of brightest Colour blaz'd.
> As blaz'd the Nut so may thy Passion grow,
> For 'twas thy Nut that did so brightly glow."
> (from Gay's "Shepherd's Week", 1714)

It was also believed that a girl who could tie a knot in the fibre from a hazel nut was sure to be married. Double hazel nuts were regarded as lucky; if you got one, you gave half to a friend, and made a wish. If a girl ate one, it was supposed that she would have twins. Carrying one in your pocket was said to protect you from toothache. Gathering nuts on Sundays and on Holy-Rood Day (14th September) was said to be dangerous, for you would meet with the Devil. ("On Holy-Rood Day the Devil goes a-nutting." - East Anglian saying, 1830)

Oak-apples: If an oak-apple was broken open, the insect found therein foretold various kinds of disaster. According to Dodoens' "Herball" (1578), the husbandmen of Kent believed that if they found an ant in an oak-apple, there would be plenty of grain; if they found a white worm, there would be cattle murrain; if they found a spider, there would be pestilence. According to Lupton's "Thousand Notable Things" (1579), if the gall-worm flew away when the oak-apple was broken open, there would be wars; if it crawled about, there would be a corn shortage; and if it ran about, there would be plague.

Rose: It was believed that if you gathered a rose on Midsummer's Day, kept it in clean white paper until Christmas Day, and then wore it in your bosom, the man who was to be your husband would come and take it out. (Devonshire, 1838; Herefordshire, 1912)

Rose-galls: These were said to cure toothache, insomnia, and whooping-cough. (Sussex, 1878; Shropshire, 1883; Wales, 1909; Herefordshire, 1912; Derbyshire, 1932)

The Sacred Grove

If you are lucky enough to have a secure and undisturbed place in which to work magic outdoors, try and build up a rapport with the spirit of the place. Tell it that you are working in harmony with the Earth, and that you will be going there regularly to perform seasonal rituals. Clear away any litter and rubbish that is dumped there, and weave the place around with protective magic. Always leave a libation of cakes and wine, or some flowers. Try and choose a place with a spring or a pool, as such places are especially magical, and sacred groves traditionally centred on a spring or a well. It is also advisable to keep the working regalia to a minimum when working outdoors, as it is difficult finding it all again in the dark. Also, you have the raw energies of nature at hand, so you just do not need as much paraphernalia to produce the right frame of mind for a ritual.

If your garden is large enough to perform rituals, you could plant herbs, trees, and symbolic flowers (see chapter on esoteric horticulture). If you do not have a garden or access to a wood, there are various trees suitable for growing indoors which can transform your temple or living room into a sacred grove, e.g. lemon (Citrus limon), orange (Citrus sinensis), fig (Ficus benjamina), ivy (Hedera helix). You can also decorate your temple with branches and garlands appropriate to the season (apple and pomegranate for Samhain; holly, ivy, and mistletoe for Yule; cherry blossom for Imbolc; pussy willow for Eostre; hawthorn for Beltane; oak for Midsummer; gorse for Lammas; apple and bramble for Autumn Equinox). You could also make Gardens of Adonis at Spring Equinox (see chapter on seasonal festivals).

Chapter 6

The Tree of Enlightenment

"The cherub with his flaming sword is hereby
commanded to leave his guard at the tree of life, and
when he does, the whole creation will be consumed, and
appear infinite, and holy, whereas it now appears finite
and corrupt.
This will come to pass by an improvement of sensual
enjoyment.
But first the notion that man has a body distinct from
his soul is to be expunged.
If the doors of perception were cleansed, everything
would appear as it is, infinite.
For man has closed himself up, and sees everything
thro' the narrow chinks of his cavern."

(from "The Marriage of Heaven and Hell" by William Blake)

The tree of life is at the heart of mystic experience in many
spiritual traditions. It is this tree which confers
enlightenment. Odin hung from the world tree for nine days
and nights; Christ hung on the Rood; Buddha sat beneath the
Bodhi tree. The tree of life is at the centre of the cosmos; it is
the immanent presence of the divine. Swinburne describes the
tree in his poem "Hertha". In this poem, the tree is the Great
Goddess, who was before time and space:

"Before ever land was,
Before ever the sea,
Or soft hair of the grass,
Or fair limbs of the tree,

173

Or the flesh-colour'd fruit of my branches, I was, and thy soul was in me."

Many poets, shamans, and mystics have envisioned the tree of life. They have got past 'the cherub with his flaming sword'. This cherub is not the winged baby of rococo art, but an angel of formidable aspect, a guardian of the threshold. Like the sphinx, this guardian of the threshold offers us riddles and enigmas. If we can solve these riddles, we can pass over the threshold into the realm of the inner self, where the Kundalini-serpent twines about the tree of life.

In the Northern Tradition, this serpent is the dragon of earth energy. The Kundalini energy, which is connected with sexuality and spirituality, is frequently suppressed in the West, and has become linked to the Shadow in the Western psyche. A common mistake is to try and kill the serpent or dragon; but like the hydra, every time one of its heads is struck off, it grows three more. In psychological terms, if you try and suppress the Shadow, it re-emerges in another form. What is needed is to integrate the Shadow into the psyche. In the earliest form of the legend of St. George, he does not kill the dragon, but places the princess's girdle around its neck. He uses the power of the Anima to control his Shadow.

In order for a spiritual tradition to be fulfilling for its adherents, it must acknowledge the Shadow, and not banish it to the outer darkness or dismiss it as evil. In the cosmology of Michael Moorcock and Roger Zelazny, the two forces in the universe are Chaos and Order (or Law). In mythology, chaos is represented by the Dragon, and order by the Hero, the Son of Light. One of the earliest forms of the combat between the hero and the dragon is the slaying of Tiamat by Marduk. When he has killed Tiamat, the Great Dragon, Marduk fashions the earth and the sky from her body. But Marduk is the son of Tiamat - in other words, chaos gives birth to order. This has been unexpectedly demonstrated by Chaos Theory, which shows that the most complex and apparently random patterns can be described mathematically.

In modern Paganism, chaos is represented by the feminine principle of growth and expansion, and order is represented by the masculine principle of death and contraction. Neither can exist without the other; each contains the seed of the other. The feminine principle is the Great Mother, the primordial tree, whose branches represent differentiation on the plane of manifestation, and whose fruit confers enlightenment and immortality. (In this context, I feel that 'immortality' represents awareness of reincarnation; one of the three kinds of knowledge acquired by the Buddha as he sat on the Immovable Spot, the centre of the universe, beneath the Bodhi Tree, was knowledge of his Life beyond lives - that is, awareness of his transcendent Self.) Within the darkness of chaos is the potentiality of light, as the Great Mother gives birth to the Child of Light; within the light there is the potentiality of darkness, as the hero must die on the tree in order to become a god. This mystery is reflected in countless myths (Attis and Cybele, Virbius and Diana, Tammuz and Ishtar, etc.).

In order to reach the Immovable Spot, it is necessary to become pure - that is, true to one's higher Self, refined to the essence of one's being. In Alchemy, this was symbolised by the transmutation of base metal into gold. The refining of metal from crude ore is a very good analogy for this process, as a pure metal simply means one which is of a single substance, not an alloy. Purity is achieved by catharsis (literally, purification), which occurs in various forms in all mystery traditions. The process of catharsis requires energy. In Alchemical terms, this is represented by the various stages in the hermetic vessel, or athanor, which produce energy.

The chakras, and the vital currents which connect them, resemble the tree of life in microcosm. In many spiritual traditions, sexual energy (associated with the lower chakras) is transmuted into spiritual energy (associated with the upper chakras). Such traditions include Alchemy, Tantra, and Witchcraft. The advantage of this approach is that it is not necessary to suppress sexuality; instead, its potential for transformation is recognised and celebrated.

Some people prefer a polygamous approach to accessing this energy, as the divine is manifest in each individual, and each sexual encounter is perceived as an encounter with the deity. According to M. Esther Harding:

> "The ritual of the virgin goddesses demanded a hieros gamos, a sacred marriage in which the woman's sexual and love life was dedicated to the goddess herself through an act of prostitution performed in the temple... the ancients felt it to be essential that every woman should once in her life give herself, not to one particular man, for love of him, that is for personal reasons, but to the goddess, to her own instinct, to the Eros principle within herself... it did not matter who the man might be, provided only that he was not the chosen man. He must be a stranger."

She goes on to say that psychological virginity (that is, independence of spirit) can only be attained by such a sacred marriage with the divine, or its embodiment. A form of hieros gamos appears to have been practised by the Tuscan witches, in the game of Benevento, where all lights were extinguished, and sexual partners were selected solely by chance.

Some, however, prefer to attain the union with the divine by means of celibacy. The mystics who were celibate had a rich inner life, as the visions of such mystics as Hildegard of Bingen show. However, celibacy must be chosen, not imposed from outside, if it is to be a source of fulfilment. In the celibate life, union with the divine occurs solely on the spiritual plane.

176

Others still prefer to attain the divine union within a monogamous relationship, the Chymical Wedding of Alchemy, or the mysterium coniunctionis. In this mystery, the physical union of the partners is mirrored by the inner union of the soul, where the Anima and the Animus join together. Fidelity is not necessitated by mere jealousy in such a relationship; rather, it follows as a natural consequence of the closeness of the union, which occurs in the hermetic vessel of the soul. Again, this situation cannot be enforced, but occurs naturally as a result of love.

Each of these paths is equally valid, and different people will choose different paths. There is a tendency to look down on people following a different path to oneself, misunderstanding the nature of other paths and the motivation of those who follow them. Whichever becomes the predominant one in any given culture or micro-culture tends to be reinforced by peer pressure. What is needed, however, is understanding and tolerance, as the imposition of a group's sexual mores onto an unwilling participant can result in great anguish, whether it be forcing a polygamous person to be monogamous, or vice versa.

Each of these paths leads to the Sacred Marriage within the psyche, provided the path is chosen in a state of awareness, not enforced by the mores of a society; and homosexual love is as much a path to the divine as heterosexual love, though the metaphysics may be different. A lesbian reverences the Goddess in the form of her lover; a gay man honours the God in the form of his lover. In some relationships, the homosexual couple may be honouring the Androgyne, which in some mythologies was the original form of humanity. Bisexuals, capable of sexual fulfilment with either gender, honour both the Goddess and the God in their relationships. As each human being has both anima and animus, capable of being fused into the androgyne, each of these forms of sexuality can produce the sexual energy which is transmuted into spiritual energy, which produces transformation in the psyche.

The transmutation of psychic energy is brought about by the performance of ritual and the exposure of the initiate to myth, which presents the interaction and development of archetypal elements in an external medium. This external spectacle is internalised by the initiate, whose internal conflicts are resolved by the cathartic myth. The association of physical reality with the spiritual realm is furthered by the sacralisation of the landscape. As each natural feature and species of flora and fauna become associated with the divine, so the awareness of the spiritual (both immanent and transcendent) is heightened. The sacral landscape is typified by the circle divided into four quarters, North, East, South, and West, corresponding to the Four Elements, the Four Seasons, the Four Winds, etc. Thus it is anchored in both time (the Four Seasons) and space (the Four Cardinal Directions). At the centre of this circle is the cosmic tree or the cosmic pillar (Yggdrasil, Irmensul, the Maypole, the Dorflinden, etc.) which often grows at the top of a hill or mountain. In ancient times, each locality had its own representation of the cosmic tree, which provided a focus for the people who lived there. According to Mircea Eliade, certain nomads carried a pole around with them, which was set up at the centre of the camp, so that wherever they were was the centre of the world. Other nomads circle around a central point, arriving at a particular place at a particular time of year, which then becomes endowed with the qualities of the season.

When the landscape is endowed with sacral qualities, we no longer feel lost in a vast uncharted territory; we become centred, and able to interact positively with the land. This does not imply jingoistic patriotism or nationalism, since any landscape can take on a sacral quality for any human being, and the same landscape can be associated with different deities by different people without conflict if there is mutual tolerance (Glastonbury Tor is an obvious example here).

It is obviously more practicable if the landscape which becomes sacred for the individual is the locality where s/he lives, since it is not particularly beneficial to be alienated from one's immediate environment. Even in urban areas, there are trees, pools, hills, and there is always the back garden, which can be endowed with sacred and mythical associations. This is achieved poetically, by metaphor and art.

"Out of the red-brown earth, out of the grey-brown streams,
Came this perilous body, cage of perilous dreams;
To the ends of all waters and lands they are tossed,
    they are whirled,
For my dreams are one with my body, yea, one with
    the world."

(from "The Earth-Child" by Gerald Gould)

The process of sacralisation is not necessarily a fully conscious one, as each place builds up associations with the moods of the beholder as it is visited at different times and seasons. If it is a place where ritual is performed, it will inevitably take on mythical associations. As communication with the spirit of place occurs, the door opens onto the realm of archetypes. As the seasons are made manifest in the cyclical changes in the landscape, the participants in the ritual become aware of the working out of mythical cycles in the wheel of the year.

In the Northern Tradition (as we have seen in Chapter 3, The Mysteries of the Forest), the sacred grove was the major centre of ritual activity; but it formed part of a landscape in which every feature was sacred. The Celtic sacred grove was centred on a pool, a well, or a spring, which was the entrance to the underworld. But each tree, stone, hill, and body of water in the landscape was sacred, and had its own spirit and its own mythology. It is still possible for the modern Pagan to interact with the sacral landscape, and to form new mythical associations with particular places. It is by this process that spirit becomes ever more immanent in matter, and the whole world is suffused with the light of the numinous.

Dane Hill, Kennett (Bronze Age Barrow)

On the hill, gazing at furrows
ploughed in the chocolate earth
I dredge the ditch of history.

Beneath my feet lie the bones
of forgotten ancestors
dreaming the land into being.

Bare-limbed trees shake in the gale,
singing an ancient song
in a forgotten language.

The furrows of earth, warm thighs,
rise and fall, breathing, in the sun,
waiting to enclose the seed.

I lie on the mound, in the grass,
dreaming with the ancestors,
at one with the land.

(Yvonne Aburrow, 7-4-94)

Chapter 7

Esoteric Horticulture: Making Your Own Sacred Grove

So twice five miles of fertile ground
With walls and towers were girdled round:
And here were gardens bright with sinuous rills;
Where blossomed many an incense-bearing tree;
And here were forests ancient as the hills,
Enfolding sunny spots of greenery.

(from "Kubla Khan" by S.T. Coleridge)

Gardens, groves, and orchards have long been the focus of ritual, a source of inspiration, a place of tranquillity, and a source of Nature's bounty. The activity of producing gardens for pleasure is almost as old as agriculture itself; the ancient Assyro-Babylonians created sacred gardens around oases, which were a pocket of green in the desert.

Many Pagans have thought about producing symbolic gardens, or gardens which are a good place for seasonal celebrations; a few ideas are offered here, including a garden for producing your own incense (a deeply satisfying activity, as home-made incense is much more personal than shop-bought varieties). Most of the garden plans given here include some trees, interspersed with herbs and flowers. Purists may be dismayed by the introduction of foreign varieties (such as Fraxinus mariesii for the Ash) but these are included as they are commercially available and suitable for garden cultivation. If you have a very large garden at your disposal, you could use the indigenous variety. Similarly, some people may disagree with my attributions of certain plants to deities, elements, planets, zodiac signs, etc. This being so, a different plant can be substituted if preferred.

Wheel of the Year Garden

Samhain:	Elder (Sambucus nigra)
	Pumpkin (Cucurbita maxima)
	Box (Buxus sempervirens)
Yule:	Holly (Ilex aquifolium)
	Chinese lanterns (Physalis alkekengi)
	Bay (Laurus nobilis)
Imbolc:	Wild cherry (Prunus avium)
	Crocus (Crocus chrysanthus)
	Snowdrop (Galanthus nivalis)
Eostre:	Goat Willow (Salix caprea)
	Primrose (Primula vulgaris)
	Daffodil (Narcissus spp.)
Beltane:	Hawthorn (Crataegus monogyna)
	Bluebell (Endymion nonscriptus)
	Violet (Viola odorata)
Midsummer:	Oak (Quercus robur)
	Flax (Linum usitatissimum)
	St. John's Wort (Hypericum perforatum)
Lammas:	Gorse (Ulex europaeus)
	Arum lily (Arum italicum)
	Field Poppy (Papaver rhoeas)
Autumn Equinox:	Apple (Malus spp.)
	Blackberry (Rubus fruticosa)
	Ivy (Hedera helix)

Key
Central feature: millstone
Stepping stones

The Wheel of the Year Garden

Lunar Garden

The flowers in this garden are either particularly fragrant by night, appear luminescent by moonlight, or are sacred to the Moon. During the day the garden is a blend of mostly blue and white flowers with interesting foliage.

Sweet cicely (Myrrhis odorata)

Lavender (Lavandula angustifolia)

Lily of the valley (Convallaria majalis)

Forget-me-not (Myosotis sylvatica)

Evening primrose (Oenothera biennis)

Foxglove (Digitalis purpurea)

White Foxglove (Digitalis purpurea 'Alba')

White stock (Matthiola incana)

Garden rue (Ruta graveolens)

White rosemary (Rosmarinus officinalis 'Albus')

Silver thyme (Thymus 'Argenteus')

Sweet rocket (Hesperis matronalis)

Moonflower (Ipomoea alba)

Glory of the Snow (Chionodoxa luciliae)

Madonna lily (Lilium candidum)

Sweet violet (Viola odorata)

White honesty (Lunaria annua)

Borage (Borago officinalis)

Mugwort (Artemisia vulgaris)

Clary Sage (Salvia sclarea)

Chicory (Cichorium intibus)

Roman wormwood (Artemisia pontica)

White Willow (Salix alba)

Spindle (Euonymus europaeus)

Lamb's tongues (Stachys lanata)

Wood anemone (Anemone nemorosa)

Winter jasmine (Jasminum nudiflorum)

Jasmine (Jasminum officinale)

Aubrieta (Aubrieta deltoidea 'Variegata')

Saxifrage (Saxifraga fortunei)

Clematis (Clematis flammula)

Snowberry (Symphoricarpos albus 'Laevigatus')

Hawthorn (Crataegus monogyna)

Irish Yew (Taxus baccata 'Fastigiata')

Bluebell (Endymion nonscriptus)

Snowdrop (Galanthus nivalis)

Silver birch (Betula alba)

Campanula (Campanula lactiflora)

Daisy (Bellis perennis)

Germander speedwell (Veronica chamaedrys)

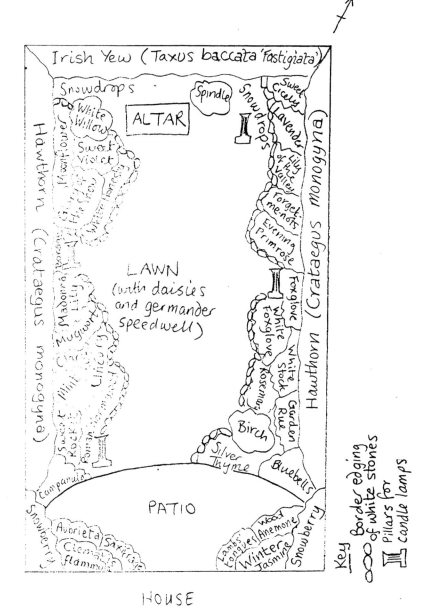

Irish Yew (Taxus baccata 'Fastigiata')

Snowdrops

White Willow

ALTAR

Spindle

Snowdrops

Sweet Cicely

Lavender

Sweet Violet

Lily of the Valley

Forget-me-nots

Evening Primrose

Foxglove

White Foxglove

White Stock

Rosemary

Garden Rue

Hawthorn (Crataegus monogyna)

Hawthorn (Crataegus monogyna)

LAWN
(with daisies
and germander
speedwell)

Madonna Lily

Mugwort

Lilies

Sweet Rocket

Pink

Roman Chamomile

Birch

Campanula

Silver Thyme

Bluebells

PATIO

Snowberry

Aubrieta

Saxifrage

Clematis flammula

Lambs' Tongues

Wood Anemone

Winter Jasmine

Snowberry

Key

Border edging
of white stones

Pillars for
candle lamps

HOUSE

The Lunar Garden

185

Solar Garden

Primarily composed of yellow, red, and orange flowers, with solar fruits such as raspberries and strawberries, this garden should appeal especially to those with Sun in Leo.

Crocus (crocus chrysanthus)

Daffodil (Narcissus spp.)

Primrose (Primula vulgaris)

Wallflower (Cheiranthus cheiri 'Cloth of Gold')

Daisy (Bellis perennis)

Snapdragon (Antirrhinum majus)

Buttercup (Ranunculus spp.)

Miniature patio rose, yellow (Rosa 'Baby Gold Star')

St. John's Wort (Hypericum perforatum)

Curry plant (Helichrysum angustifolium)

Welsh poppy (Menocopsis cambrica)

Leopard's bane (Doronicum plantagineum)

Jerusalem Sage (Phlomis fruticosa)

Pansy, yellow (Viola x wittrockiana 'Golden Champion')

Larkspur, yellow (Delphinium 'Butterball')

Marigold (Tagetes erecta)

Variegated spindle (Euonymus fortunei 'Emerald 'n' Gold')

Golden privet (Ligustrum ovalifolium 'Aureo-marginatum')

Mountain Laurel (Kalmia latifolia)

Strawberry (Fragaria x ananassa)

Raspberry (Rubus idaeus)

Chinese lantern (Physalis alkekengi)

Red-hot poker (Kniphofia uvaria)

Sunflower (Helianthus annuus)

Orange buddleia (Buddleia globosa)

Rosemary (Rosmarinus officinalis)

Basil (Ocimum basilicum)

Sweet Marjoram (Origanum majorana)

Golden Thyme (Thymus x citriodorus 'Aureus')

Sage (Salvia argentea)

Parsley (Petroselinum crispum)

Winter jasmine (Jasminum nudiflorum)

Broom (Cytisus scoparius)

Forsythia (Forsythia x intermedia)

Hazel (Corylus avellana)

Holly (Ilex aquifolium)

Feverfew (Tanacetum parthenium)

Nasturtium (Tropaeolum majus)

Tansy (Tanacetum vulgare)

Bay (Laurus nobilis)

Smoke bush (Cotinus coggygria 'Royal Purple')

Wild Cherry (Prunus avium)

Bachelor's Buttons (Kerria japonica)

Crocosmia (Crocosmia x crocosmiiflora)

Coral flower (Heuchera sanguinea)

The Solar Garden

Four Elements Knot Garden 1

Northern Tradition

Air, Black, North:
    Irish Ivy (Hedera helix 'Hibernica')
    Black Hellebore (Helleborus niger)
    Purple Sage (Salvia horminum 'Blue Bouquet')

Fire, Red, East:
    Cotoneaster (Cotoneaster adpressus)
    Madder (Rubia tinctorum)
    Arum lily (Arum italicum)
    Fly Agaric (Amanita muscaria)

Earth, White / Yellow, South:
    Spindle (Euonymus fortunei 'Silver Queen')
    St. John's Wort (Hypericum perforatum)
    Tansy (Tanacetum vulgare)
    Daisy (Bellis perennis)
    Autumn Crocus (Crocus ochroleucus)

Water, Green / Blue, West:
    Blackthorn (Prunus spinosa 'Plena')
    Borage (Borago officinalis)
    Green Alkanet (Pentaglottis sempervirens)
    Bluebell (Endymion nonscriptus)

Trees:
    Holly (Ilex aquifolium) - Winter
    Birch (Betula pendula) - Spring
    Rowan (Sorbus aucuparia) - Summer
    Hazel (Corylus avellana) - Autumn

Hazel nuts

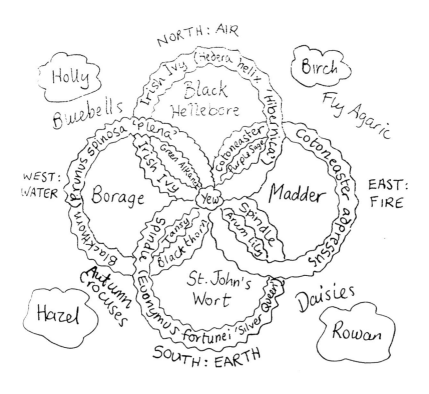

Four Elements Knot Garden 1 - Northern Tradition

Four Elements Knot Garden 2

Western Tradition

Air, Yellow, East: Golden Sweet Bay (Laurus nobilis 'Aurea')

Marigold (Calendula officinalis)

Lavender (Lavandula officinalis)

Ash (Fraxinus mariesii)

Fire, Red, South: Wintergreen (Gaultheria procumbens)

Red lupin (Lupinus 'Cherry Pie')

Nasturtium (Tropaeolum majus)

Holly (Ilex aquifolium)

Water, Blue, West: Bog myrtle (Myrica gale)

Borage (Borago officinalis)

Green Alkanet (Pentaglottis sempervirens)

Willow (Salix alba)

Earth, Green, North: Dwarf box (Buxus sempervirens 'Suffruticosa')

Lovage (Levisticum officinale)

Basil (Ocimum basilicum)

Walnut (Juglans regia)

Ash

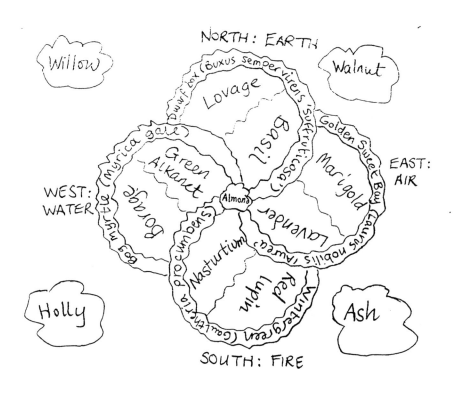

Four Elements Knot Garden 2 - Western Tradition

Astrological Garden

East (Air):   Whitebeam (Sorbus aria)
South (Fire):   Holly (Ilex aquifolium)
West (Water):   Common Willow (Salix cinerea)
North (Earth):   Irish Yew (Taxus baccata 'Fastigiata')

Aries: Rosemary (Rosmarinus officinalis)
            Cowslip (Primula veris)
            Garlic (Allium sativum)

Taurus: Apple Mint (Mentha rotundifolia)
            Thyme (Thymus vulgaris)
            Coltsfoot (Tussilago farfara)

Gemini: Caraway (Carum carvi)
            Dill (Anethum graveolens)
            Lavender (Lavandula officinale)

Cancer: Agrimony (Agrimonia eupatoria)
            Lemon Balm (Melissa officinalis)
            Daisy (Bellis perennis)

Leo: Marigold (Calendula officinalis)
            Borage (Borago officinalis)
            Chamomile (Anthemis nobilis)

Virgo: Savory (Satureia montana)
            Valerian (Valeriana officinalis)
            Fennel (Foeniculum vulgare)

Libra: Violet (Viola odorata)
            Pennyroyal (Mentha pulegium)
            Yarrow (Achillea millefolium)

Scorpio: Basil (Ocimum basilicum)
            Tarragon (Artemisia dracunculus)
            Wormwood (Artemisia pontica)

Sagittarius: Musk Mallow (Malva moschata)
            Feverfew (Tanacetum parthenium)
            Sage (Salvia horminum 'Blue Bouquet')

Capricorn: Solomon's Seal (Polygonatum x hybridum)
            Comfrey (Symphytum officinale)
            Sorrel (Rumex acetosa)

Aquarius: Mullein (Verbascum thapsus)
            Fumitory (Fumaria officinalis)
            Silver Thyme (Thymus 'Argenteus')

Pisces: Rose, miniature (Rosa 'Eleanor')
            Meadowsweet (Filipendula ulmaria)
            Lungwort (Pulmonaria officinalis)

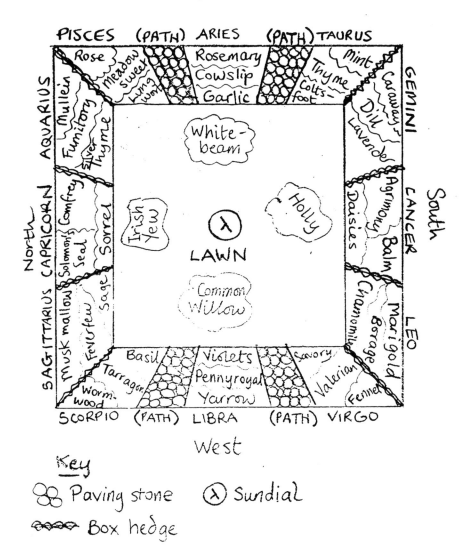

The Astrological Garden

Planetary Garden

Sun: Spruce (Picea abies)   Mars: Dogwood (Cornus alba 'Sibirica')
          Sunflower (Helianthus annus)   Jupiter: Oak (Quercus robur)
Moon: Willow (Salix Cinerea)   Saturn: Holly (Ilex aquifolium)
Venus: Rose (Rosa rubrifolia)
Mercury: Ash (Fraxinus mariesii)
          Rowan (Sorbus aucuparia)

Hedges: Dwarf box (Buxus sempervirens 'Suffruticosa')
         Grey Santolina (Santolina chamaecyparissus)

Bed 1:   Jasmine (Jasminum officinale)
(Yin)   Apple Mint (Mentha rotundifolia)
         Thyme (Thymus vulgaris)
         Rosemary (Rosmarinus officinalis)
         Sage (Salvia argentea)
         Dill (Anethum graveolens)

Bed 2:   Winter Jasmine (Jasminum nudiflorum)
(Yang)   Basil (Ocimum basilicum)
         Tansy (Tanacetum vulgare)
         Garlic (Allium sativum)
         Chives (Allium schoenoprasum)
         Tarragon (Artemisia dracunculus)

Bed 3:   Pear (Pyrus communis)
(Yin)   Silver Thyme (Thymus 'Argenteum')
         Lavender (Lavandula officinalis)
         Madonna lily (Lilium candidum)
         Lily-of-the-valley (Convallaria majalis)

Bed 4:   Apple (Malus spp.)
(Yang)   St. John's Wort (Hypericum perforatum)
         Leopard's Bane (Doronicum plantagineum)
         Daffodil (Narcissus spp.)
         Primula (Primula vulgaris)
         Crocus (Crocus aureus)

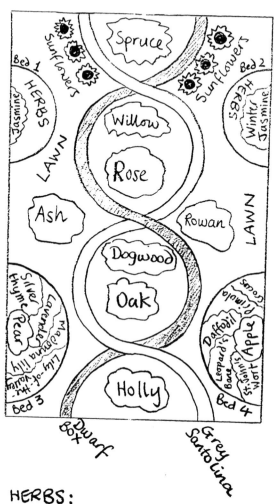

Bed 1
Sunflowers
HERBS
Jasmine
LAWN
Spruce
Sunflowers
Bed 2
HERBS
Winter Jasmine
Willow
Rose
Ash
Rowan
LAWN
Dogwood
Oak
Silver thyme Pear
Lavender
Madonna lily
Lily-of-the-valley
Daffodil
Leopard's Bane
St. John's Wort
Pimelo Grows
Apple
Bed 3
Bed 4
Holly
Dwarf Box
Grey Santolina

HERBS:
Mint, Thyme, Basil, Rosemary, Tansy,
Sage, Garlic, Chives, Dill, Tarragon, etc.

The Planetary Garden

Grail Garden

The flowers in this garden have been chosen either for their association with the Grail legend (Periwinkle, Lily, Bee Balm), their cup-shaped flowers, or their colour (red for wine and blood, white for the Virgin goddess, blue for the Moon, purple for royalty).

Black snake-root (Cimicifuga racemosa)
Crocus (Crocus tomasinianus)
Narcissi (Narcissus 'Mount Hood')
Crocosmia (Crocosmia masonorum)
Madonna lily (Lilium candidum)
Heuchera (Heuchera sanguineum)
Clematis (Clematis x 'Jackmanii Superba')
Rose (Rosa rubrifolia)
Peach-leaved bellflower (Campanula persicifolia)
Large periwinkle (Vinca major)
Small white periwinkle (Vinca minor 'Alba')
Guelder Rose (Viburnum opulus)
Wormwood (Artemisia pontica)
Rue (Ruta graveolens)
Hyssop (Hyssopus officinalis)
Bay (Laurus nobilis)
Basil (Ocimum basilicum)
Sage (Salvia horminum 'Rose Bouquet')
Borage (Borago officinalis)
Bee balm (Monarda didyma)
Rosemary (Rosmarinus officinalis)
Rose (Rosa longicuspis)
Wisteria (Wisteria sinensis)
Fuchsia (Fuchsia magellicana, syn. F. macrostemma)
Jasmine (Jasminum officinale)
Polygonum (Polygonum amplexicaule 'Atrosanguineum')
Myrtle (Myrtus communis)
Lobelia (Lobelia erinus 'Mrs. Clibran')
Sword lily (Gladiolus byzantinus)
Campanula (Campanula lactiflora)
Snowdrop (Galanthus nivalis)   Hosta (Hosta fortunei 'Aureomarginata')
Poppy (Papaver rhoeas)   Almond (Prunus dulcis)

Feature: stone, cup, fountain, or cauldron

The Grail Garden

Ogham Garden

Beech hedge (Fagus sylvaticus) - a good dense hedge which provides privacy.

Black hellebore (Helleborus niger)	- Air
Madder (Rubia tinctoria)	- Fire
St. John's Wort (Hypericum perforatum)	- Earth
Borage (Borago officinalis)	- Water

Beth	Birch (Betula pendula)
Luis	Rowan (Sorbus aucuparia)
Fearn	Alder (Alnus glutinosa)
Saille	Willow (Salix cinerea)
Nuin	Ash (Fraxinus excelsior)
Huath	Hawthorn (Crataegus mongyna)
Duir	Oak (Quercus robur)
Tinne	Holly (Ilex aquifolium) or Holm Oak (Quercus ilex)
Coll	Hazel (Corylus avellana)
Quert	Apple (Malus sylvestris)
Muin	Bramble (Rubus fruticosa)
Gort	Ivy (Hedera helix)
Ngetal	Reed (Phragmites communis)
Straif	Blackthorn (Prunus spinosa)
Ruis	Elder (Sambucus nigra)
Ailm	Elm (Ulmus glabra)*
Onn	Gorse (Ulex europaeus)
Ur	Heather (Erica carnea)
Eadha	Aspen (Populus tremula)
Ioh	Yew (Taxus baccata)

* I have substituted Wych Elm (Ulmus glabra) for the more correct Common Elm (Ulmus procera) because of Dutch Elm Disease.

Beech hedge

Black Hellebore
Yew
Birch
Rowan
Madder
Aspen
Alder
Heather
Willow
Gorse
Ash
LAWN
Elm
FIRE PIT
Haw-thorn
Elder
Oak
Black thorn
Holly
Hazel
Borage
Reed
Ivy
Bramble
Apple
St. John's Wort

W

E

S

KEY
⟨◌◌◌⟩ Stones

NOTES

Reeds (Ngetal) will need a small pond.
Bramble (Muin) will need to be trained.
Heather (Ur) needs acidic soil.
Ivy (Gort) will need to be trained.

The Ogham Garden

Runic Garden

N.B. Plants marked with an asterisk are POISONOUS. This garden is not recommended if you have children.

Feoh	Nettle (Urtica dioica)
Ur	Iceland moss
Thorn	House leek (Sempervivum tectorum)
Os	Magic mushroom or Liberty Cap (Psilocybe semilanceata) *
Rad	Mugwort (Artemisia vulgaris)
Ken	Cowslip (Primula veris)
Gyfu	Pansy (Viola tricolor)
Wyn	Flax (Linus usitatissimum)
Haegl	Black bryony (Tamus communis) *
Nyd	Snakeroot (Cimicifuga racemosa)
Is	Henbane (Hyoscyamus niger)
Ger	Rosemary (Rosmarinus officinalis)
Eoh	White bryony (Bryonia alba) *
Peordh	Aconite (Eranthis hyemalis)
Elhaz	Sedge (Carex spp.)
Sigel	Juniper (Juniperus communis)
Tyr	Purple sage (Salvia farinacea)
Beorc	Lady's Mantle (Alchemilla mollis)
Eh	Ragwort (Senecio jacobea)
Man	Madder (Rubia tinctoria)
Lagu	Leek (Allium porrum)
Ing	Self-heal (Prunella vulgaris)
Odal	Clover (Trifolium repens)
Daeg	Sage (Salvia nemorosa)
Ac	Tormentil or Thormantle (Potentilla tormentilla)
Aesc	Fly Agaric (Amanita muscaria) *
Yr	Mandrake (Mandragora officinalis) *
Ior	Ivy (Hedera helix) *
Ear	Hemlock (Conium maculatum) *
Cweorth	Rue (Ruta graveolens)
Calc	Yarrow (Achillea millefolia)
Stan	Blackthorn (Prunus spinosa)
Gar	Ash (Fraxinus excelsior); Garlic (Allium sativum)

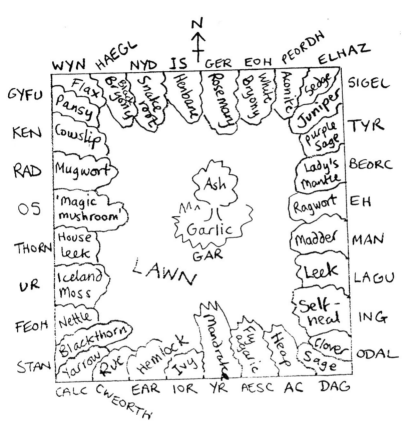

A yew hedge could be grown around the edge if privacy is required.

The Runic Garden

Yggdrasil Garden

The lawn is intended to represent the night sky with stars, hence the use of blue and white flowers. The flower beds represent the nine worlds of Yggdrasil. Midgard is represented by a central lawn with daisies, and Jormungand, the Midgard serpent, by ivy on the edge of the lawn.

LAWN

Yew (Taxus baccata 'Dovastoniana')

Apple (Malus sylvestris)

Whitebell (Endymion nonscriptus)

Star of Bethlehem (Ornithogalum umbellatum)

Forget-me-not (Myosotis sylvatica)

Daisy (Bellis perennis)

Hazel (Corylus avellana)

Alder (Alnus glutinosa)

Bluebell (Endymion nonscriptus)

Germander Speedwell (Veronica chamaedrys)

Green Alkanet (Pentaglottis sempervirens)

Asgard:

Ash (Fraxinus mariesii)

Black bryony (Tamus communis)

Red wallflower (Cheiranthus cheiri 'Blood Red')

Sweet woodruff (Galium odoratum)

Berberis (Berberis darwinii)

- Yggdrasil

- Air

- Fire

- Earth

- Water

Midgard:

Daisy (Bellis perennis)

Irish Ivy (Hedera helix 'Hibernica')

Niflheim:

Rowan (Sorbus aucuparia)

Silver thyme (Thymus 'Argenteus')

Lamb's tongue (Stachys lanata)

Curry plant (Helichrysum angustifolium)

Bifrost:

Red primula (Primula vulgaris)

Yellow primula (Primula vulgaris)

Blue primula (Primula vulgaris)

Purple primula (Primula vulgaris)

Orange primula (Primula vulgaris)

Green: Hosta (Hosta sieboldiana)

Mauve primula (Primula vulgaris)

Muspellheim:
Red tulip (Tulipa 'Shakespeare', Division 12)   Red Salvia (Salvia splendens)
Field Poppy (Papaver rhoeas)

Vanaheim:
Chamomile (Anthemis nobilis)   Hawthorn (Crataegus monogyna)
Dog rose (Rosa canina)

Svartalfheim:
White mugwort (Artemisia lactiflora)   Dwarf Box (Buxus sempervirens
Rue (Ruta graveolens)   'Suffruticosa')

Lightalfheim:
Spindle (Euonymus fortunei 'Emerald 'n' Gold)   Mandrake (Mandragora officinalis)
Golden thyme (Thymus x citriodorus 'Aureus')

Jotunheim:
White lavender (Lavandula angustifolia 'Alba')   White rosemary (Rosmarinus
White foxglove (Digitalis purpurea 'Alba')   officinalis 'Albus')

Ice bridge:
White honesty (Lunaria annua)

Hel:
Black nightshade (Solanum nigra)
- you can use the Chilean Potato Tree (Solanum crispum 'Autumnale') which is not
poisonous, instead, if you prefer:

Sage (Salvia horminum 'Blue Bouquet')   Bryony (Bryonia alba)

Rosa Alba

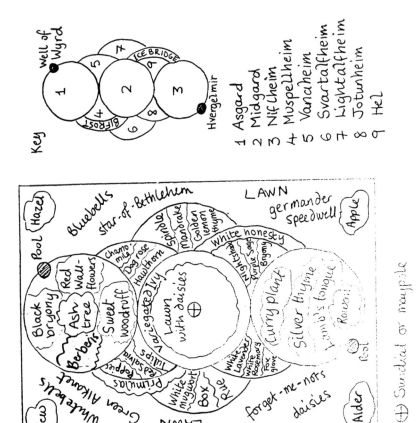

Key

Well of Wyrd

ICE BRIDGE
BIFROST

Hvergelmir

1 Asgard
2 Midgard
3 Nifheim
4 Muspellheim
5 Vanaheim
6 Svartalfheim
7 Lightalfheim
8 Jotunheim
9 Hel

LAWN
germander
speedwell

Apple

Pool (Hazel)
Bluebells
star-of-Bethlehem

Spindle
Mandrake
Golden lemon thyme
White honesty

Chamomile
Dog rose
Hawthorn

Nightshade
Purple Sage
Bryony

Black bryony
Red Wall-flowers

Ash tree
Sweet woodruff

Variegated ivy

Lawn with daisies

Curry plant
Silver thyme
Lamb's tongue
Rowan

Barberis

Tulips
Red salvia
Primulas
Poppies

White mugwort
Box
Rue

White Lavender
White Rosemary
Fox glove

forget-me-nots
daisies

Root

Yew
Whitebells
Green Alkanet

LAWN

Alder

⊕ Sundial or maypole

The Yggdrasil Garden

Incense Garden 1

For Container Growing

Patio Rose (Rosa 'Eleanor')	- Venus
Bay (Laurus nobilis)	- Sun
Lemon (Citrus limon) *	- Moon
Orange (Citrus sinensis) *	- Sun
Juniper (Juniperus communis)	- Fire, Jupiter
Strawberry (Fragaria x ananassa)	- Venus
Onion (Allium cepa)	- Mars
Garlic (Allium sativum)	- Fire, Mars
Jasmine (Jasminum officinale)	- Moon
Ivy (Hedera helix)	- Earth, Saturn
Hops (Humulus lupulus)	- Mars
Sunflower (Helianthus annuus)	- Sun
Wormwood (Artemisia pontica)	- Fire
Aniseed (Pimpinella anisum)	- Air, Mercury
Balm of Gilead (Cedronella canariensis)	- Air, Jupiter
Poppy (Papaver rhoeas)	- Water, Moon
Sweet Cicely (Myrrhis odorata)	- Water
Ginseng (Panax ginseng)*	- Earth
Orris (Iris florentina)	- Earth
Fennel (Foeniculum vulgare)	- Mercury
Valerian (Valeriana officinalis)	- Mercury
Ginger (Zingiber officinalis)*	- Fire, Mars
Mint (Mentha x piperita)	- Mars
Rosemary (Rosmarinus officinalis)	- Sun
Basil (Ocimum basilicum)	- Mars
Lavender (Lavandula officinalis)	- Air
Chamomile (Anthemis nobilis)	- Leo, Sun
Lovage (Levisticum officinale)	- Venus
Violet (Viola odorata)	- Venus

* Pots may need taking indoors in winter and on cold nights

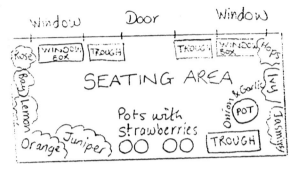

PATIO OR BALCONY

Contents of troughs:

Sunflower
Wormwood
Aniseed
Balm of Gilead
Poppy
Sweet Cicely
Ginseng
Orris
Fennel
Valerian

Contents of window boxes:

Ginger
mint
Rosemary
Basil
Lavender
Chamomile
Thyme
Lovage
Violet

The Incense Garden 1

Incense Garden 2

For an Ordinary Garden

As for Garden 1 plus:

Willow (Salix cinerea)	- Water, Moon
Wild Cherry (Prunus avium)	- Air
Cedar ((Cedrus libani 'Nana')	- Fire
Pine (Pinus mugo)	- Earth
Eucalyptus or Alpine Snow Gum (Eucalyptus niphophila)	- Saturn
Almond (Prunus dulcis)	- Venus
Climbing rose (Rosa longicuspis)	- Venus
Lilac (Syringa vulgaris)	- Jupiter
Opium poppy (Papaver somniferum)	- Water, Moon
Tansy (Tanacetum vulgare)	- Sun
Jack-by-the-hedge (Alliara petiolata)	- Mars
Marigold (Calendula officinale)	- Sun
Dittany (Dictamnus albus)	- Earth
Vervain (Verbena officinalis)	- Venus

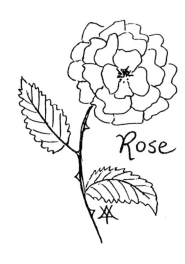

Rose

Willow

Access to Lawn is under trees.
(Willow, Wild Cherry, Cedar, Pine)

The Incense Garden 2

Sumerian Garden

The trees are all sacred to Sumerian deities. The pool represents the Apsu, the underground sea of Sumerian legend. The cedar is the Sumerian world tree. The flowers in the beds are blue, symbolising the lapis lazuli of Ishtar's necklace.

Willow (Salix cinerea)	- symbol of Inanna
Poplar (Populus alba)	- symbol of Inanna
Cedar (Cedrus libani)	- sacred to Dumuzi
Cypress (Cupressus sempervirens)	- sacred to Dumuzi

Jasmine (Jasminum officinale)	- sacred to the Moon
Rose (Rosa rubrifolia)	- sacred to Venus
Bay (Laurus nobilis)	- sacred to the Sun

Periwinkle (Vinca major)
Sword lily (Gladiolus byzantinus)
Columbine (Aquilegia discolor)
Larkspur (Delphinium tatsienense)
Lobelia (Lobelia erinus 'Crystal Palace')
Campanula (Campanula lactifolia)
Bluebell (Endymion nonscriptus)
Borage (Borago officinalis)

Jasminum officinale

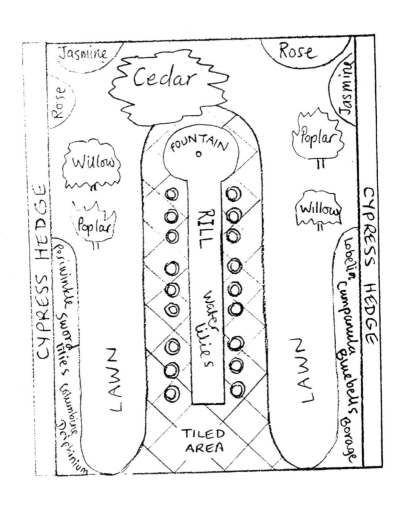

Key
○○○ Pots with bay trees

Sumerian Garden

Appendix One

Surnames and Place Names Possibly Indicating Pagan Activity or Sacred Trees

Surnames: Oak, Nokes, Noakes, Alder, Nalder, Ash, Nash

Celtic tribal names: Eburones, Eburovices (yew, Ibor); Lemovice (elm)

Place names:

Alderley
Alderton
Aller
Allerby
Aller Dean
Allerford
Allerston
Allerthorpe
Allerton
Allhallows (?)
Amberley
Annesley
Ansley
Apley
Appley
Appleton Thorn
Asgarby
Ashley
Ashwell
Avebury
Aveley
Badwell Ash
Bardsey
Bardsley
Bardwell
Barrow
Beacontree
Beech
Belthorn
Birch
Birchgrove
Blackcraig Hill
Blackhill
Blackley
Boxgrove
Boxley
Bransly Hill (?)
Bride
Bridestowe
Brideswell
Broad Oak
Broom

Broome
Bucks Horn Oak
Burry Holms
Cairn
Coven
Coveney
Covenham
Crabtree
Dore Holm
Druid
Druidale
Druidston
Ealing (ealh Ing?)
Elm
Elmbridge
Elmdon
Elmhurst
Elmley Castle
Elmswell
Elveden
Fair Oak
Fir Tree
Five Ashes
Five Oaks
Garstang
Garswood
Gorsedd Bran
Gorsley
Great Maplestead
Grimeford Village
Grime's Graves (Grim was a by-name of Woden)
Grimes Hill
Grimethorpe
Grimley
Grimsargh
Grimsay
Grimsby
Grimscote
Grimscott
Grimsthorpe

Grimston
Grimstone
Grove
Gwalchmai
Hagley
Hawthorn
Hawthorn Hill
Hazel Grove
Hazeley
Hazelrigg
Hearthstane (?)
Helford
Helstone
Herne (Kent)
Hernhill (Kent)
Holmsgarth
Holywell
Horne
Horn Hill
Hornsey
Ingbirchworth
Ingrave
Ings
Ingworth
Maplebeck
Mapledurham
Mapledurwell
Maplehurst
Mapleton
Maplin Sands
Maybole
Mayfield
May Hill
Mayland
Maypole
Maypole Green
Nash
Nine Ashes
Nine Barrow Down
Noak Hill
Noke
North Fearns

Oakdale
Oake
Oaken
Oakgrove
Oakhill
Oakley
Odin Bay
Odstone
Okehampton
Pooksgreen
Puckington (?)
Sevenoaks
Shire Oak
Shireoaks
Six Ashes
Stanghow (?)
Temple (?)
Thorne
Thorney
Thornhill
Thornley
Thornthwaite
Thorns
Thurne
Thurnham
Thursley
Wansdyke (Wodens dic, 903)
Wednesbury
Wednesfield
Wenslow, Beds.
(Woden's mound)
Woodnesborough
(Wodnesbeorge, 1086)
Witcham
Witchampton
Witchford
Withypool
Woodhenge

211

Appendix Two

Roman Priests

The three major priests at Rome were the priests of Jupiter, Mars, and Quirinus. A priest was called a flamen (plural flamines). There were twelve other priests for various other deities, as follows:

DEITY	PRIEST	FESTIVALS
Jupiter	Flamen Dialis	13th September; Ides of November
Mars	Flamen Martialis	1st, 14th, & 23rd March
Quirinus	Flamen Quirinalis	
Volturnus	Flamen Volturnalis	
Pales	Flamen Palatualis	21st April
Furria	Flamen Furrinalis	25th July
Flora	Flamen Floralis	28th April - 3rd May
Falacer	Flamen Falacer	
Pomona	Flamen Pomonalis	
Volcanus	Flamen Volcanalis	
Ceres	Flamen Cerialis	19th April
Carmentis	Flamen Carmentalis	11th & 15th January
Portunus	Flamen Portunalis	

The flamines were priests of individual gods and looked after their temples. The flamen Dialis (priest of Jupiter) was surrounded by taboos, because he was an embodiment of Jupiter. These taboos included not being allowed to touch or name ivy, a goat, a dog, raw meat, or beans; not being allowed to walk under a vine; only having his hair cut by a free man with a bronze knife; and his hair and nails, when cut, had to be buried beneath a lucky tree. His wife, the Flaminica, had to observe much the same rules, with some additional ones specific to her, such as offering an expiatory sacrifice if she heard thunder.

The costume of the flamines was archaic; they wore an apex (a conical or round cap surmounted by a piece of pointed olive wood and surrounded at its base by a strand of wool), a laena (a thick woollen cloak fastened with a bronze fibula), and a laurel wreath.

Appendix Three
Anglo-Saxon tree names

Anglo-Saxon	Modern name(s)	Latin
ac	Oak	Quercus robur
aesp, aeps, aepse	Aspen	Populus tremula
alor	Alder	Alnus glutinosa
anan beam	Spindle	Euonymus europaeus
apuldor	Apple	Malus sylvestris
birce	Birch	Betula pendula
brembel, bremel	Bramble	Rubus fruticosa
brer	Briar	Rosa spp.
cwicbeam	Rowan (or may be Mountain Elm or Aspen	Sorbus aucuparia Ulmus montana Populus tremula)
elebeam	Olive	Olea sativa
ellen	Elder	Sambucus nigra
elm	Elm	Ulmus spp.
eow	Yew	Taxus baccata
ful-beam	Alder Buckthorn	Frangula alnus

gate-treow	Dogwood (or may be Willow	Cornus spp. Salix spp.)
haesel	Hazel	Corylus avellana
hnut-beam	nut-tree	(probably hazel)
holen	Holly	Ilex aquifolium
ifig	Ivy	Hedera helix
lithwyrt	Wayfaring Tree	Viburnum lantana
mapuldor	Maple	Acer campestre
mistel, mistel-tan	Mistletoe	Viscum album
oleastrum, wilde elebeam	Sea Buckthorn, Oleaster, Wild Olive	Hippophae rhamnoides
sealh	Sallow	Salix cinerea
slahthorn	Blackthorn, Sloe	Prunus spinosa
welig	Willow	Salix spp.
wice	Wych-elm	Ulmus glabra
withig	Withy	Salix spp.
wudubind[e]	Woodbine, Honeysuckle	Lonicera spp.

Appendix Four

Magical Uses of Trees

Protection

Trees which are used for protection are: ash, bay, buckthorn, coconut, cypress, elder, gorse, hawthorn, hickory, holly, ivy, larch, mistletoe, mulberry, oak, palm, pepper tree, plum, pomegranate, quince, rose, rowan, sandalwood, wild service, wayfaring tree, and witch-hazel.

Healing

Trees which are used in healing spells are: ash, aspen, bramble, horse chestnut, elder, eucalyptus, and lime (the fruit).

Invocation

Trees used for summoning spirits are: alder, bamboo, buckthorn, and yew.

Purification

Trees which are used in purification are: bay, birch, bramble, broom, cedar, gum arabic, lemon, osier, tamarisk, and willow.

Fertility

Trees used in fertility magic are: banana, birch, coconut, fig, mistletoe, oak, olive, orange, palm, pine, pomegranate, quince, and willow.

Divination

Trees used for divinatory magic are: apple, ash, hazel, orange, poplar, rowan, and witch-hazel. These can all be used for making Runes for use in divination (except perhaps orange and witch-hazel, which would be very difficult to obtain, and are not indigenous species).

Love

Trees used in love spells are: apple, apricot, avocado, brazil, cherry, sweet chestnut, lemon, papaya, plum, prickly ash, rose, walnut, and willow.

N.B. Love spells should only be used to encourage love, never to coerce someone into loving. For example, if two people obviously love each other but seem unable to communicate this, it is acceptable to give them a helping hand; likewise if a relationship is foundering due to lack of communication, a spell to facilitate this would be acceptable. Where the practitioner of magic is not a partner in the relationship, it is prudent to act only at the request of one or preferably both of the partners. If the practitioner of magic is a partner in the relationship, she or he should ask the other partner if he or she is willing. Some love spells involve finding out who your partner will be. This is inadvisable, since when you meet them your assumption that they will feel the same way may put them off altogether! It should also be noted that the karmic effects of coercive or inappropriate love spells last for seven years - the first six months are sheer hell, but the other six and a half years are not very nice either, so think VERY carefully before attempting any kind of love spell, even non-specific spells to attract a lover.

If you think you have been the victim of a love-spell, make use of the protective trees. The Arabs believe that eating pistachio nuts will break a love-spell, so try that as well.

Money

Trees used in spells for prosperity are: almond, horse chestnut, and gorse.

N.B. Spells for money or jobs should not specify the source of the money or job, since someone else may need that particular money or job more than you do. However, general prosperity spells are acceptable, provided they are not motivated by greed or laziness, but come from a genuine need.

The categories listed above are intended as a reference to refer the reader to the more detailed entries in the Tree Index.

PLANETARY RULERSHIPS

Incense makers, herbalists, and practitioners of magic may find the following list of planetary rulerships helpful:

Sun (principle of self-integration): balsam, bay, benzoin, cashew, cedar, citron, frankincense, grapefruit, gum arabic (acacia), hickory, juniper, hemlock tree, lime (fruit), mistletoe, olibanum, orange, palm, pine, spruce, thuja, walnut, witch-hazel.

Mercury (principle of communication): almond, ash, cassia, hazel, mace, mulberry, pecan, pistachio, pomegranate, rowan.

Venus (principle of unity, love, and friendship): apple, apricot, avocado, banana, birch, bramble, cananga, cherry, damson, elder, guelder rose, hornbeam, magnolia, peach, pear, persimmon, plum, rose, rosewood, spindle, wayfaring tree, whitebeam, ylang-ylang.

Mars (principle of action; phallic, warlike): dogwood, gorse, hawthorn, larch, pepper tree, prickly ash.

Moon (rhythmic principle: instinct, intuition, dreams): alder, aspen, bamboo, bergamot, broom, cassia, coconut, jasmine, lemon, linaloe, myrrh, olive, opoponax, osier, papaya, privet, sallow, sandalwood, willow.

Jupiter (principle of expansion, learning, and wisdom): banyan, blackthorn, bo tree, cajeput, sweet chestnut, horse chestnut, clove, fig, fir, lime or linden, field maple, great maple, niaouli, nutmeg, oak, plane, ti tree.

Saturn (principle of contraction, limitation, formation): beech, buckthorn, elm, eucalyptus, holly, ivy, mimosa, poplar, quince, tamarind, tamarisk, wild service, yew.

Pluto (principle of transformation through elimination and renewal): box, cypress.

Neptune (refining principle): ash.

Uranus (principle of deviation and invention): cedar.

Chiron (principle of healing: the Wounded Healer): ash, aspen, elder, eucalyptus.

When cutting fruit, leaves, boughs, twigs, nuts, etc. from trees it is customary to leave an offering to the spirit of the tree. Magic is said to work by the law of returns, that is, a gift requires a gift. Acceptable offerings include a vow of action, money, food, a libation, or at the very least, a prayer of thanks. (Vows could include promises to do something for the environment.)

In the case of money obtained by magical means, a portion of it should be spent on the poor and needy by the recipient, in order to share the benefit; otherwise the gods will not be so willing to grant your request the next time.

INCENSE

Smell is the most evocative of all the senses. Who has not stood among myrtle bushes on a hot day, and breathed in the pleasing scent; been reminded of their grandmother's house by the smell of new-baked bread; or had their senses uplifted by the subtle perfume of incense?

Many magical rituals require incense. In "The Sea Priestess" by Dion Fortune, the priestess kindles the Fire of Azrael, for insight into past lives. It consisted of juniper, sandalwood, and cedarwood. An incense can be made from these trees, using 1 oz sandalwood chips, 1 oz crushed juniper berries, and 10 drops essential oil of cedarwood, or, if you can get them, a green cedar cone (ground up small enough to burn), or some cedarwood chips.

Other ingredients of incense derived from trees are: willow bark, Gum Arabic (from the acacia tree), olibanum (from any tree of the genus Boswellia), oak bark, bay leaves, pine resin, cassia, bamboo, rose, jasmine, mistletoe, hemlock tree resin, ivy, rowan leaves and berries, opoponax, myrrh, frankincense, cassia, cinnamon, clove, nutmeg, mace, jasmine, balsam, ylang-ylang, lemon, lime, orange, rosewood, mastic, and cypress.

Cypress is burned as an incense to allay grief and to help heal invalids; the greenery from the tree can be dried and used as incense.For example, Cedar incense is used for purification and getting rid of bad dreams; Juniper incense is used by the Tibetans to expel demons; Mistletoe is burnt to ward off evil; Pine is used for purification; Rose petals are used in healing incenses; Rowan leaves and berries are added to divination incenses, along with bay leaves; and Gum Arabic is used for spirituality and purification.

TALISMANS

Talismans are a form of 'contagious magic', that is, they are charged magical objects carried on the person. Many people carry 'lucky charms' for stressful situations; these are a sort of 'mass-produced' talisman. Most talismans produced by a practitioner of magic, however, will be purpose-made for the occasion. If you are going to make your talisman from wood, it is a good idea to use an appropriate wood for the purpose, by referring to the lists of planetary correspondences and magical uses above, and to make an appropriate offering to the tree. The talisman is then carved with runes or planetary symbols (but not both - eclectic synthesis weakens the effect) and a phrase expressing the purpose for which the talisman is intended. Then the talisman is magically charged, invoking the appropriate deity.

Planetary Tree.

APPENDIX 5

Useful addresses

Alarm UK: The Alliance Against Road-building (promotes radical grass-roots campaigning). New members receive information pack on campaigning. Membership costs £10 p.a. and includes the newsletter Alarm Bells. Alarm UK, 13 Stockwell Road, LONDON, SW9 9AU. (071 737 6641)

British Trust for Conservation Volunteers (BTCV): Carries out practical conservation work in rural and urban areas. BTCV, 36 St. Mary's Street, Wallingford, Oxon., OX10 0EU. (0491 39766)

CPRE: Council for the Protection of Rural England (a long-standing pressure group for a variety of countryside issues including quarrying and road-building). CPRE, Warwick House, 25 Buckingham Palace Road, LONDON, SW1W 0PP.

DRAGON (eco-pagan action group) c/o Adrian Harris, 3 Sanford Walk, New Cross, LONDON, SE14 6NB.

Earth First! (Radical eco-activists - contact your local group)

Friends of the Earth: all environmental issues. For details, contact your local FoE group, or write to FoE, 26-28 Underwood Street, LONDON, N1 7JQ.

Henry Doubleday Research Association (organic horticulture, information, and seeds). HDRA, National Centre for Organic Gardening, Ryton-on-Dunsmore, Coventry, CV8 3LG. (0203 305317)

Survival International (promotes the rights and culture of tribal peoples). Survival International, 310 Edgware Road, London, W2 1DY. (071 723 5535)

Transport 2000 (promotes use of alternative eco-friendly forms of transport). Transport 2000, 3rd floor, Walkden House, 10 Melton Street, LONDON, NW1 2EJ. (071 388 8386)

Tree Council (promotes tree-planting, organises National Tree Week). Tree Council, 35 Belgrave Square, London SW1. (071 235 8854)

The Woodland Trust (saves an average of a wood a week, and protects over 580 areas throughout the country) The Woodland Trust, Autumn Park, Grantham, Lincolnshire, NG31 6LL.(0476 74297)

Bibliography and Further Reading

Yvonne Aburrow,   "The Enchanted Forest: the Magical Lore of Trees", Capall Bann
     Publishing, 1993.
Margaret Baker,   "Folklore and Customs of Rural England", David and Charles, 1974.
Brian Bates,   "The Way of Wyrd", Arrow Books, 1987.
Henry Bett,   "English Myths and Traditions", Batsford, 1952.
Bruno Bettelheim,   "The Uses of Enchantment: The meaning and importance of fairy tales",
     Penguin, 1991.
Lesley Bremness,   "The Complete Book of Herbs", Dorling Kindersley, 1992.
K. M. Briggs,   "The Anatomy of Puck: an examination of Fairy beliefs among
Shakespeare's contemporaries and successors", RKP, 1959.
Katharine M. Briggs, "A Dictionary of British Folk-Tales", Vols. 1 & 2, Routledge and
     Kegan Paul, 1970.
Joseph Campbell,   "The Inner Reaches of Outer Space: Metaphor as Myth and as Religion",
     Harper Perennial, 1988.
Jean-Paul Clebert, "The Gypsies", Pelican Books.
J. C. Cooper (ed.), "Brewer's Book of Myth and Legend", Helicon,1993.
K. Crossley-Holland, "British Folk Tales: new versions", Orchard
          Books, 1987.
Nicholas Culpeper,   "Culpeper's Complete Herbal", Foulsham.
S. Cunningham,   "Encyclopedia of Magical Herbs", Llewellyn,1989.
Georges Dumezil,   "Archaic Roman Religion" (trans. Philip Krapp), Uni. of Chicago Press,
     1970.
L. Durdin-Robertson, "The Year of the Goddess: A Perpetual Calendar of Festivals",
     Aquarian Press, 1990.
J. & S. Farrar,   "The Witches' Goddess: the feminine principle of divinity", Hale, 1987.
J. & S. Farrar,   "The Witches' God: Lord of the Dance", Hale, 1989.
Eric L. Fitch, "In Search of Herne the Hunter", Capall BAnn Publishing, 1994.
J. G. Frazer,   "The Golden Bough: A Study in Magic and Religion", abridged edn.,
     Macmillan, 1983.
S. O. Glosecki,   "Shamanism and Old English Poetry", Garland,1989.
Mrs. M. Grieve,   "A Modern Herbal", Tiger Books, 1931, 1973, 1993.
A. J. Gurevich,   "Categories of Medieval Culture" (trans. G. L. Campbell), Routledge &
     Kegan Paul, 1985.
M. Esther Harding,   "Woman's Mysteries, Ancient and Modern", Shambhala, 1990.
Thomas Hinde,   "Forests of Britain", Victor Gollancz, 1985.
Robert Holdstock, "Mythago Wood", Grafton, 1986
Robert Holdstock, "Lavondyss", Gollancz, 1988.
Christina Hole,   "English Folk Heroes", Batsford, 1948.
W. G. Hoskins,   "The Making of the English Landscape", Hodder & Stoughton, 1955.
Glyn Hughes,   "The Hawthorn Goddess", Penguin, 1985.
Glyn Hughes,   "The Antique Collector", Sceptre, 1991.
Ronald Hutton,   "The Pagan Religions of the Ancient British Isles: Their Nature and
     Legacy", Blackwell, 1991.
Ronald Hutton,   "The Rise of Merrie England" (forthcoming).
Nigel Jackson, "The Call of the Horned Piper", Capall Bann Publishing, 1994.
Evan John Jones,   "Witchcraft: A Tradition Renewed", Hale, 1990.
Michael Jordan,   "Gods of the Earth", Bantam Press, 1992.
Evan John Jones,   "Witchcraft: A Tradition Renewed", Hale, 1990.
G. & T. Jones (trans.), "The Mabinogion", Everyman, 1978.
Paul Kay,   "Incense: An Idiot's Guide" (booklet)

Charles Kightly, "The Customs and Ceremonies of Britain: An Encyclopedia of Living Traditions", Thames and Hudson, 1986.

Rudyard Kipling, "Puck of Pook's Hill", Piccolo, 1975.

Rudyard Kipling, "Rewards and Fairies", Penguin Classics, 1987.

Jacques Le Goff, "The Medieval Imagination" (trans. A. Goldhammer), Uni. of Chicago Press, 1988.

F. Marian MacNeill, "The Silver Bough", Canongate Clasic (no. 24) 1956, 1989.

Naomi Mitchison, "The Corn King and the Spring Queen", Canongate Classics (no. 29), 1931, 1990.

R. M. Ogilvie, "The Romans and their Gods", Chatto & Windus (Ancient Culture and Society), 1969.

Nigel Pennick, "Practical Magic in the Northern Tradition",Aquarian Press, 1989.

Nigel Pennick, "The Secret Lore of Runes and Other AncientAlphabets", Rider, 1991.

Nigel Pennick, "Runic Astrology: Starcraft and Timekeeping in the Northern Tradition", Aquarian Press, 1990.

F. Perring, A. Gagg, "The Macmillan Field Guide to Wild Flowers", M. Walters, Macmillan, 1989.

Michael John Petry, "Herne the Hunter: A Berkshire Legend", Wm. Smith (Booksellers) Ltd

John Rodgers, "The English Woodland", Batsford, 1941.

Anne Rooney, "Hunting in Middle English Literature",Brewer, Cambridge, 1993.

Anne Ross, "Pagan Celtic Britain", Constable, 1992.

N. K. Sandars (trans. & ed.), "The Epic of Gilgamesh", Penguin Classics, 1975.

H. H. Scullard, "Festivals and Ceremonies of the Roman Republic", Thames and Hudson, 1981.

William Shakespeare, The Complete Works.

Robin Skelton & "Earth, Air, Fire, Water: Pre-Christian and Pagan Margaret Blackwood, Elements in British Songs, Rhymes, and Ballads", Arkana, 1990.

R. J. Stewart, "Where is Saint George? Pagan imagery in English Folksong", Blandford Press, 1988.

R. J. Stewart, "Celtic Gods, Celtic Goddesses", Blandford,1990.

Godfrid Storms, "Anglo-Saxon Magic", Nijhoff, The Hague, 1948.

F. H. Swanson & "Herb Garden Design", University Press of New England, 1984.
V. B. Rady,

A. C. Swinburne, "Selected Poems" (ed. L. M. Findlay), Fyfield Books, 1982.

J. R. R. Tolkien (trans.), "Sir Gawain and the Green Knight; Pearl; Sir Orfeo", Allen & Unwin, 1979.

Rosemary Verey, "Rosemary Verey's Garden Plans", Frances Lincoln, 1993.

Brian Wicker, "The Story-shaped World", Athlone Press, 1975.

Steve Wilson, "Robin Hood: The Spirit of the Forest", Neptune Press, 1993.

Edgar Wind, "Pagan Mysteries in the Renaissance", OUP,1980.

B. Woledge, G. Brereton, & A. Hartley, "The Penguin Book of French Verse", Penguin,1977.

Encyclopedia of Garden Plants and Flowers, Reader's Digest Books,1987.

New Larousse Encyclopedia of Mythology, Larousse, 1985.

Index

FREE DETAILED CATALOGUE

A detailed illustrated catalogue is available on request, SAE or International Postal Coupon appreciated. **Titles can be ordered direct from Capall Bann, post free in the UK** (cheque or PO with order) or from good bookshops and specialist outlets. Titles currently available include:

Angels and Goddesses - Celtic Christianity & Paganism by Michael Howard
Arthur - The Legend Unveiled by C Johnson & E Lung
Auguries and Omens - The Magical Lore of Birds by Yvonne Aburrow
Book of the Veil The by Peter Paddon
Caer Sidhe - Celtic Astrology and Astronomy by Michael Bayley
Call of the Horned Piper by Nigel Jackson
Celtic Lore & Druidic Ritual by Rhiannon Ryall
Earth Dance - A Year of Pagan Rituals by Jan Brodie
Earth Magic by Margaret McArthur
Enchanted Forest - The Magical Lore of Trees by Yvonne Aburrow
Familiars - Animal Powers of Britain by Anna Franklin
Healing Homes by Jennifer Dent
Herbcraft - Shamanic & Ritual Use of Herbs by Susan Lavender & Anna Franklin
In Search of Herne the Hunter by Eric Fitch
Magical Guardians - Exploring the Spirit & Nature of Trees by Philip Heselton
Magical Lore of Cats by Marion Davies
Magical Lore of Herbs by Marion Davies
Masks of Misrule - The Horned God & His Cult in Europe by Nigel Jackson
Patchwork of Magic by Julia Day
Psychic Self Defence - Real Solutions by Jan Brodie
Sacred Animals by Gordon MacLellan
Sacred Grove - The Mysteries of the Forest by Yvonne Aburrow
Sacred Geometry by Nigel Pennick
Sacred Lore of Horses The by Marion Davies
Sacred Ring - Pagan Origins British Folk Festivals & Customs by Michael Howard
Seasonal Magic - Diary of a Village Witch by Paddy Slade
Secret Places of the Goddess by Philip Heselton
Talking to the Earth by Gordon Maclellan
Taming the Wolf - Full Moon Meditations by Steve Hounsome

Capall Bann is owned and run by people actively involved in many of the areas in which we publish. Our list is expanding rapidly so do contact us for details on the latest releases.

Capall Bann Publishing, Freshfields, Chieveley, Berks, RG20 8TF